Forged Metal Ballerina.

CREATING WITH METAL

K. E. GRANSTROM

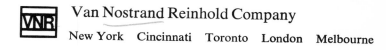

Van Nostrand Reinhold Company

New York   Cincinnati   Toronto   London   Melbourne

Van Nostrand Reinhold Company Regional Offices:
New York   Cincinnati   Chicago   Millbrae   Dallas

Van Nostrand Reinhold Company International Offices:
London   Toronto   Melbourne

Printed in Great Britain by Jolly and Barber Ltd, Rugby,
Warwickshire.

Published by Van Nostrand Reinhold Company
450 West 33rd Street, New York, N.Y. 10001

Published simultaneously in Canada by
Van Nostrand Reinhold Ltd.

16 15 14 13 12 11 10 9 8 7 6 5 4 3

Contents

Foreword 5

Part 1 WORKSHOP TECHNIQUES 6
The Hobby Workshop 6
Equipping the Workshop 7
Purchasing Tools 10
Tools 10

MATERIALS 18
Silver and Gold 19
Copper 19
Copper Alloys 20
Aluminum 21
Zinc.................... 21
Tin..................... 21
Lead.................... 21
White Metal (Babbitt Metal) .. 22
Iron 22

MATERIALS—SIZES
AND SHAPES 23
JOINING METHODS 23
Soft Soldering 23
Hard Soldering............. 25
Riveting 27
Screw Joints 29

SURFACE TREATMENT...... 31
Polishing 31
Cleaning 31
Etching 31
Coloring 33
Tinning 33
Lacquering 34
Enameling 34
Chasing 35

Part 2 WORKING DRAWINGS
AND MODELS—
EASY MODELS 36
Small Items (Shelf Supports,
Drawer Handles, Padlock
Mounting) 36
Corner Reinforcement 38
Pencil Holder 38
Paperweight 39
Ink Blotter 39
Shelf Brackets............. 40
Tool Holders 40
Bunsen Burner 41
Soldering Iron 42

Part 3 WORKING DRAWINGS
AND MODELS—
MORE DIFFICULT
MODELS............... 42
Letter Openers 44
Forming and Raising
Bowls and Cups 47
Salad Set and Serving Spoon .. 54
Napkin Rings 55
Bracelets 56
Brooches 61
Earrings 64
Necklaces 67
Pulling Wire............. 68
Mirror Frames 69

Part 4 SMITHING OR FORGING.... 71

FORGING—WORKING
DRAWINGS AND
MODELS............... 74
Fireplace Pokers 75
Candlestick—Model 1 77

Candlestick—Model 2 80

Slit Decoration 81

Double Candlestick 83

Wall Sconce—Model 1 84

Wall Sconce—Model 2 85

Ballerina 87

Bootscraper Dog 88

Fish 89

Ornamental Door Knocker . . . 90

Furniture Hardware 91

SURFACE TREATMENT
  OF FORGED ARTICLES . . 92

Part 5 FURTHER EXAMPLES 94

Witches' Cauldron 94

Hinge 95

Lamp 96

Lampstand 98

Chandelier 99

Horse 100

Bull 101

Owl 102

Fish 103

Crow 104

Flock of Birds 105

Adam and Eve 106

Oxen 107

Tree Trunks 108

Bootscraper Dog forged on the anvil.

Foreword

Many hobbyists think that metalworking is a craft only for those who are fortunate enough to have a fully equipped machine shop and a large stock of tools. Nothing could be more incorrect. A number of metalworkers consistently use very primitive equipment and a few favorite tools. Naturally, just as in any other craft, it requires a certain minimum of tools to work metal but you can create some very attractive articles with surprisingly little equipment.

Anyone who has had the opportunity of seeing an Oriental village craftsman at work will know that they seem to produce the most beautiful metal objects almost magically out of thin air. Sitting on the bare earth in front of his primitive hut, he will work with only a few large nails and a crude lump of iron, used as a hammer. For an anvil, he will use his thigh or knee. Nevertheless, the finished work is so handsome and well-shaped that tourists are eager to buy them. Beautiful handwork made with the fewest possible tools and under the most simple conditions always brings forth our admiration and envy. The skill of these primitive craftsmen is ample proof that mechanical aids and expensive tools are not essential for creating with metal.

Most metals, beautiful in themselves, become even more handsome when they are worked, ground, buffed, and polished. It is a completely engrossing material to work with, and a wonderfully satisfying and relaxing change of pace to sit in a cozy hobby room and putter around with wire, sheet metal, fire, and soldering gear.

Metal may seem to be a somewhat obstinate material until you have learned, with a little experience, just how to judge the many different forms a particular piece can take. Naturally, you will make mistakes at first, but you will learn from each experiment. Of course your beginning projects should certainly not be in expensive silver. Use readily available tin food cans to work a number of experimental objects to gain confidence.

The designs in this book have been selected to inspire the beginner, as well as the more experienced craftsman, to make objects which are both decorative and useful, yet which can be completed in a comparatively short period of time.

Part I

Workshop Techniques

The Hobby Workshop

Naturally it is ideal to have a fully equipped workshop and some enthusiastic hobbyists do invest in elaborate installations, but this is not necessary. Many hobbyists will simply avail themselves of the dining room or kitchen table and will have to be content with working on a rather small scale, for they will have to be careful not to scratch or cut the furniture while working and must invariably spend a lot of time each work session in cleaning away the unavoidable disorder of filing and cutting metal parts. Any small room where you can work on your hobby and leave the project undisturbed until the next session is preferable to a large, but temporary, work area.

It is a good idea for the amateur to see how professional craftsmen arrange their shops. He may be surprised to find out that even master craftsmen will sometimes have their workshops in small cellars or in gloomy backyard sheds. Because many high-quality handicrafts come from such dreary places, one must conclude that happiness in creating means more to a craftsman than a fine workshop. In other words, since it is the desire to create that impels the work, if you really want to do metalwork, you will certainly be able to find some place to do it, no matter how cramped and restricted the space.

Should you have a large house with a roomy basement, you will be able to select and equip a good workshop area very well. But whether you own a house with a basement, an attic, an outdoor shed, a garage, or simply an apartment with some storage space, you must have easy access to the work area so that you can bring in and store any necessary large pieces of material such as long metal rods and bars. You will find it is much cheaper to buy materials in quantity rather than in small bits and pieces.

How should one start a good metalworking workshop? Large windows and a good artificial light source are essential. You should also have one or two lights near the vise, and an electric outlet nearby for an extension lamp.

The workroom should have a good floor. Although a concrete floor is usable, it should be insulated with linoleum, cork, or vinyl. For a real workshop, however, this type of flooring is not tough enough. Install a real wood floor which you can lay yourself, using planed, tongue-and-groove lumber of inexpensive 1″ pine boards nailed to sleepers placed approximately 20″ to 24″ apart on the concrete floor which has first been covered with asphalt paper. If necessary, adjust the sleepers with wedges so that the flooring will be level and even. This kind of wood floor is not expensive, and you need not cover the entire area; a wooden walkway along the workbench is sufficient.

For cold winter climates, cover raw concrete cellar walls with insulation board attached to 1″ x 2″ wood studs. Doors and windows can be weather-stripped. Some type of small heater should be available for your comfort in cold weather.

Equipping the Workshop

A most important item for the metal workshop is a solid *workbench*.

You can make one of 1¼″ or 2″ stock lumber nailed to a solid 4″ stock lumber frame. Most people can work comfortably at a table that is about 36″ high, however you should find a height most satisfactory for yourself. The width of the tabletop may be about 24″ but, of course, this will depend on the dimension of the planks you are using. It is easier to use the whole plank and not have to trim down the last one. After planing the top surface of the table planks, screw a length of angle iron along the entire front edge of the table to protect it from being nicked and cut as you work.

The back and rear legs of the table should be fastened solidly to the wall with angle irons and expansion bolts or wall plugs, using large wood screws. As the workbench must be rigid, attach the front legs solidly to the floor if possible.

A bench vise should be fastened to the workbench. Since a good strong vise is quite expensive, many amateurs may be tempted to buy a cheaper one that is too small and too weak, usually made of inferior material. A vise with parallel jaws, 5″ to 6″ wide, is cheaper in the long run and better-suited for most hobby jobs. For working with small objects you can also use a hand vise.

To avoid getting the cross-file marks of the bench vise jaws on fine pieces such as jewelry or finely polished metal, you can buy protective vise jaw covers.

The workshop must be equipped with some type of *anvil*. A real smith's anvil is best since it has sharp edges and one or two horns for shaping flat iron, etc. However, you can work with a good sized cross-section of a train rail,

for instance. The anvil is used as a support in forming, riveting, chiseling, and bending the work.

Place the anvil either on the flat surface of the worktable or, preferably, on a special cutting block with a flat, smooth, end surface. The cutting block is best, particularly for a smith's anvil. If you position the anvil on the worktable, place it directly above one of the legs, which is the strongest spot.

You now have the basic equipment for a metalworking hobby shop. Of course, you will need some hand tools; the variety will depend on the projects you are planning to undertake and the amount of money you have to spend.

A cross-section of railroad track makes a practical anvil.

You can buy an electric or hand-powered *drill*. The drill chuck should be able to hold rather large drills, at least up to ½″. An electric drill which comes with a stand so that it can be used as a stationary bench drill is preferable, but so expensive that most amateurs have to be satisfied with the cheaper hand drills.

For the drill you will need a set of metal-working drill bits, from 1/32″ up to the maximum your drill will take. The variation between the different drill bit sizes may be 1/32″, or 1/64″ for the smaller drills.

A *brace and bit* is used exclusively for woodworking. The chuck on a brace and bit cannot normally hold a cylindrical metalworking drill bit, and for this reason alone, you should not be tempted to purchase this inexpensive tool. It is also too clumsy and uncomfortable for metalwork.

Sooner or later most hobbyists will buy a *grinding wheel* for sharpening the metal drills, chisels, etc., and again your budget will dictate whether it be electric or hand-powered.

Other necessary tools will include: *pliers, tongs, wrenches, screwdrivers, hammers, chisels, metalworking saws, files, mandrels, center punch*, etc. The total cost of these small hand tools will be fairly high, but you can, of course, buy them only as you need them.

In order to get the most out of your hobby shop, you must not be satisfied with just buying equipment that "will do." Look around and get long-lasting tools of good quality.

The best method of arranging your tools is that used by professional craftsmen, on a large, open *tool board*. This can be made from planed tongue-and-groove planking with hooks screwed into it for handily hanging up each and every tool. There should be enough space to accommodate new tools as you buy them.

Tools should be hung in groups according to their use—and, for example, screwdrivers can be hung in a row according to size. Hooks and hangers of many types are available at hardware stores or can be devised at home.

When your tools are hung up on the board, draw a line silhouette around each one with black cellulose lacquer to indicate where it belongs. You can then quickly see if any tool is missing from the board. Cover the board with a few coats of clear lacquer or varnish.

An easy way to make a tool board is to use pegboard. Despite its rather thin appearance, pegboard is very strong, made of hard, oil hardened pressed wood-fiber sheet and provided with evenly spaced, pre-cut holes. Sometimes obtained with a plastic finish on one side, pegboard usually comes in a soft, natural brown surface which can be painted with ordinary oil or plastic paints. You can buy all sorts of hooks, to be inserted in the holes of the pegboard, at your hardware or dime store. Available in large sheets at the lumber yard, pegboard can be cut to your specific requirements.

The electric hand drill should never be left connected to the electric outlet. Suspend the chuck of the drill from one of the larger hooks on the board for safe and easy storage. The electric soldering iron, which may still be hot, should never be left attached to an outlet, but should be placed on two special hooks screwed into the workbench.

Gradually you are bound to accumulate a number of small items such as screws, bolts, nuts, rivets, etc., and you will need some orderly storage place for them. Set up dividers in a handy *drawer* and keep the articles of different lengths and sizes in separate compartments. You might paste labels on the outside of this drawer, listing the contents.

Adjustable bench vise for mounting on the workbench. They are available on turntables—to be set into any position—then locked.

Loose covers can be mounted on the vise jaws, as seen in the drawing, to protect softer, polished metals as they are worked.

You can also buy several transparent *compartmentalized boxes,* or attach a group of clear screw-top glass jars with 2 nails through the top to the *underside* of a shelf over the worktable. The glass is simply unscrewed when necessary and the metal top remains fixed to the shelf. You can also use a swing-container which consists of a number of clear plastic boxes meant to hold spices or cereals and which are arranged on a stand so that they can be swung out, one by one. This stand is easily screwed to the wall or worktable.

You will also need a place to store your raw materials, metals, and half-finished pieces. Bookcases, primitive wall shelves supported by angle irons, or floor-to-ceiling wood strips with several shelves nailed to them, are all equally suitable.

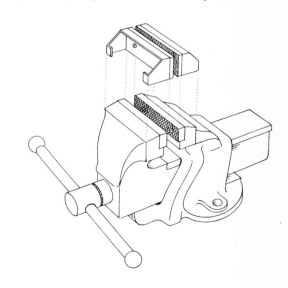

Purchasing Tools

Tools are to be carefully collected. At first buy only what you need in order to get started. It is foolish to buy a tool for which you have *no immediate need*. When you start working with metal you will soon realize which tools are really necessary and which you can do without. You will be more satisfied with a tool collection in which each piece has been purchased for a specific purpose, than with one cluttered with tools indiscriminately bought on sale at the local hardware store.

Each tool should be selected for the task it is to perform; it is false economy to purchase inferior, cheap tools. Quality tools, although naturally somewhat more expensive, last indefinitely and are much easier to work with than poor tools.

An experienced craftsman can tell at a glance if a tool is as good as it looks (or is advertised), which an amateur cannot. He must use other methods. Examine the tool itself. Does it feel good in your hand? Does it carry the name of a reputable manufacturer? Good quality tools always have the manufacturer's name stamped on them in a clearly visible place. Be suspicious of a tool which does not carry the manufacturer's name. Finally, look at the general appearance and surface. If, for example, pliers are "decorated" with a thick layer of brightly colored lacquer, you can be fairly sure that they will not last long. The lacquer is not there only to attract customers by bright colors, but really to hide a poor grade of steel or a poorly finished surface.

The best tools are always made of fine grade steel carefully selected at the factory according to the tool's intended use. The surface is finely ground and polished so that the tool is pleasing to handle. The working surface is hard-ened to the correct degree. If too hard it would break, and if not hard enough, it would dull too easily.

Buying tools made by a large factory known for its quality products is almost always a safe venture, for you will have a piece of equipment that you can use year after year.

Tools

Tools should be correctly *handled* and carefully *maintained*.

You will learn to use tools properly as you work with them. The first rule is to use the tool only for the job it is intended to do, and for nothing else. For example, do not use a screwdriver as a hammer, a metalworking drill as a center punch, or a tap as a file. If you let such bad habits become established you will soon ruin your entire collection of tools, whether they are of high quality or poor. Each tool, having been constructed for a specific purpose, can be expected to last a reasonable length of time only if it is employed especially for this purpose alone.

Good maintenance actually begins with the tool storage. Order must be maintained in the hobby workshop. Hang tools up on a tool board. Do not allow them to lie around on the workbench or toss them haphazardly into a drawer. Cutting tools such as files, drills, and chisels will become dull very quickly with improper care.

We cannot go into specific directions for the care of every tool in this book, but we can recommend that you keep your eyes open and notice the way in which a good craftsman handles his tools. You can learn a lot by watching a good machine worker sharpen a metal drill. This is, by the way, one of the

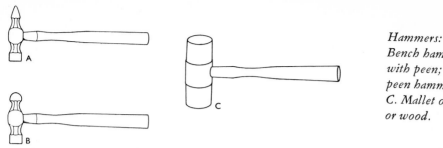

Hammers: A. Bench hammer with peen; B. Ball-peen hammer; C. Mallet of rubber or wood.

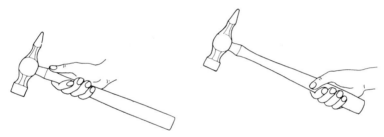

How to use the bench hammer: The one at the left is held incorrectly. Diagram at the right shows the proper grip.

most difficult tasks for an amateur to learn on his own. Do not hesitate to ask a craftsman for advice. Most artisans are proud of the craft they have learned and like to explain its intricacies.

Hammers should be the type that machine and metal craftsmen use. The carpenter's claw hammer is unsuitable for metalworking. A small bench hammer with a peen and a similarly proportioned ball peen hammer are considered necessary for metalworking. The hammer shaft should be made of ash or hickory wood securely wedged onto the hammer head with a steel wedge or thin wooden wedge. Never use the hammer shaft for hitting, not even in places impossible to reach with the hammer. Protect soft metals and polished surfaces with a supporting layer of wood or use a mallet of wood, lead, plastic, or rubber. The work at hand will determine the proper weight and size of the hammer to use. Blows from a very heavy hammer can cause serious and permanent changes in the shape of the metal. Using a hammer that is too light for more heavy work will completely ruin it. Certain metalwork will require special hammers.

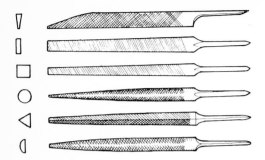

Files are the most frequently used tools in metalcraft. You should work with a file so that its teeth remove some of the metal when they are pressed down and moved forward against the material. Selecting the appropriate file depends on the metal's hardness and toughness, on how much metal is to be removed, on the size of the surface to be worked, and on the finished appearance desired.

Files are available with teeth of various degrees of coarseness; for example, there are rough, bastard, second cut, and smooth files. Rough and smooth files are the most common. A single-cut file gives the finest, smoothest, and most even surface, while a double-cut file bites better and removes more metal per stroke. Riffle files are used for small jobs on surfaces that are difficult to reach. Use needle files for small holes and edges. For fastening in a machine-drill chuck there are several types of drills in different shapes which will file or mill specific holes, grooves, etc., in a moment.

With use, shavings and dirt will eventually clog up the teeth of a file. Clean with a special file brush (file card, or cleaner), and not with just any available nail or steel wire. If the file has been used on wood (a practice to be avoided), shavings can be removed from the teeth by placing the file in warm water for a moment to make the shavings swell up. After-

wards they can easily be removed with a file brush. A new file is often smeared with oil to prevent rust. Remove the oil by rubbing the file with chalk or charcoal to absorb the grease, which can then be brushed away.

Put a handle on a new file as soon as you get it, for you should never use the file without a handle, as the sharp point can seriously injure your hand. Drill a hole in the handle for the file shank (the smooth, triangular-shaped pointed end). Measure the file shank at its largest dimension, and drill a short hole exactly in the center of the handle with a drill of the same diameter as the file shank. Continue the drilling with a smaller drill. Finally, drive the handle firmly onto the shank.

When filing you should hold the file with both hands, your right hand around the handle, and your left around the file point. The piece on which you are working must be firmly placed in the vise. Guide the file forward with a calm, even pressure. Do not press down when you are drawing the file back or you will damage its teeth.

Hacksaws for cutting metal come in several sizes. Your hacksaw should have detachable blades with teeth of varying coarseness. Coarse teeth are good for coarse work, and fine teeth for sheet metal, thin-walled pipe or tubes, etc. The coarseness of the blade is determined by the number of teeth per inch. The best blades are made of high-speed steel.

The piece of metal must be firmly fastened in the vise as close to the cutting line as possible, and the hacksaw, like the file, must be guided forward with a light pressure and pulled backward without pressure. Fasten the blade taut in the hacksaw frame before use and loosen it again after the work is finished.

Wrenches are tools for tightening or loosening nuts and bolts. Several popular wrenches can be adjusted to fit various nut sizes. These wrenches are not as good as fixed-end wrenches, but are adequate for the beginner. Other types of wrenches are the open-end wrench, socket wrench, and box-end wrench, which are far beyond the needs of the amateur. Fixed-end wrenches, which are usually made of vanadium alloy steel, are very durable and strong, but relatively expensive.

Screwdrivers are employed to loosen and tighten notched machine screws. You must have several screwdrivers, because they must exactly fit the grooves or notches of varying lengths and widths in the heads of machine screws. They should be made of vanadium steel. The handle can be of a synthetic (plastic) or wood, and must be set firmly on the stem.

Metalworking drills are spiral grooved and are only used for drilling holes in metal. The best ones are of high-speed steel.

A new drill which is sharp, drills a nice circular hole in the metal, but after the drill has been used several times it becomes dull and must be sharpened. Sharpen metal drills on a not-too-hard grinding wheel which rotates at a high speed. A novice may find sharpening a drill point in the correct way, difficult. Briefly, as little as possible should be ground off and the drill's original cutting angle should be preserved. You absolutely must not grind a drill either too pointed or too flat. Finally, if the centering (balance) is destroyed, the drill will turn crookedly. Grinding gauges are available to facilitate the task for beginners.

Before beginning to drill, mark the exact point to be drilled with a center punch. If the spot is not deeply marked, the drill cannot grab hold.

Professional wrenches: A. Box-end wrench; B. Open-end wrench; C. Crescent wrench; D and E. Sockets; F. Socket wrench and handle.

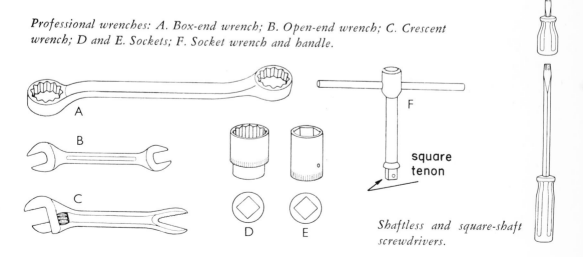

square
tenon

Shaftless and square-shaft screwdrivers.

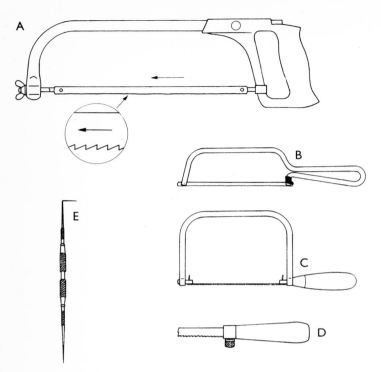

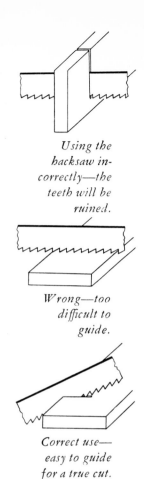

Using the hacksaw in-correctly—the teeth will be ruined.

Wrong—too difficult to guide.

Correct use—easy to guide for a true cut.

Saws: A. Hacksaw (circled directions show proper insertion of the blade); B. Junior, or small-size hacksaw; C. Coping saw for cutting metal; D. Keyhole saw; E. Scriber, or engravers' tool for marking metal.

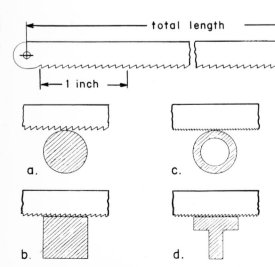

total length

1 inch

a.

b.

c.

d.

Diagram at left shows the hacksaw blade. The four enlarged views below show various degrees of coarseness in the blades. For cutting soft steel use blade a, with 14 teeth per inch; for tooled steel, use blade b, 18 teeth per inch; for pipe and tubes, blade c, 32 teeth per inch; and for cutting profiles, use blade d, with 24 teeth per inch.

Metal drills should be stored in a special case with separate pockets for each drill size. You may want to buy or make one of the practical wood racks designed for these drills. Drill bits are placed upright in holes so that they are easy to select while you work.

Pliers come in different shapes, such as flat nose, pointed nose, round nose, end nippers, diagonal cutting pliers, etc. Use these for firmly holding the piece to be worked and for small bending jobs. Occasionally apply a drop of oil in the joint of the pliers.

approx. 118°

Normally, the cutting surfaces of a metal-working drill bit (even after grinding), should form an angle of about 118°.

Chisels for metal are used in the same way as a mortise chisel on wood, i.e., for splitting, cutting in two, carving, and chipping. Cross-cut chisels and flat chisels are the most popular kind.

Grinding wheels for hobby use can be the hand-driven type. It's important that the grinding wheel is firmly tightened on the shaft and correctly adjusted. If a grinding wheel is "heavy" on one side it will shake and rotate unevenly, and you risk having it break apart at high speeds. You can buy various lead shims and washers to adjust the balance.

Taps and dies are used for cutting threads in metal. For interior threads in holes, use taps. Usually you use three different taps for one thread cutting. Begin with a pointed tap, continue with a center tap, and finish with an end tap.

A hole in which threads are to be cut should be worked with a drill of somewhat smaller diameter than the screw to be used in the threaded hole.

Cut outside threads with dies which are mounted in a special holder (diestock, or wrench). Using a piece of round iron tubing of 1/4" diameter, you can directly cut 1/4" threads on its outer side. In cutting outside threads the piece and the finished threads must have the same diameter, unlike cutting an inside threading.

When you cut threads, use the age-old method of "two steps forward and one step back." This helps you by releasing the tension of the tools for threading and also by preserving the condition of the taps and dies. Cutting the threads must be done slowly and carefully. Some metals must be smeared with a special cutting oil—common machine oil cannot be used for this.

15

The use of screws, nuts, and rivets is explained later, in the section on joining.

This brief discussion about metalworking tools doesn't pretend to be complete. It is merely an orientation. Tool catalogs are an excellent source of information and completely describe available tools for any specific job. There is one very important point to remember: All tools *must* constantly be protected against rust. Cultivate the habit of rubbing tools with an oiled cloth (kept at hand) immediately after use. If rust spots appear, scrape them off immediately with an emery cloth, and recondition the metal by rubbing it well with oil. There are some heavier oils which contain rust-proof agents and these can be used beneficially, if the tool is not to be used for some time. Always be on the alert for rust, for it can spoil a good tool in an amazingly short period of time.

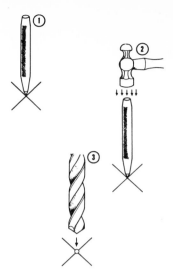

Three steps for marking a drilling position. Draw a cross with the scriber, place the center punch at the intersection point of the X (1). Hit the punch with a hammer several times (2), to make an indentation in which to start the drill (3).

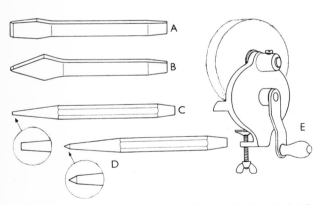

Chisels: A. Flat chisel; B. Cross chisel; C. Mandrel (flat point); D. Center punch; E. Hand-powered grinding wheel.

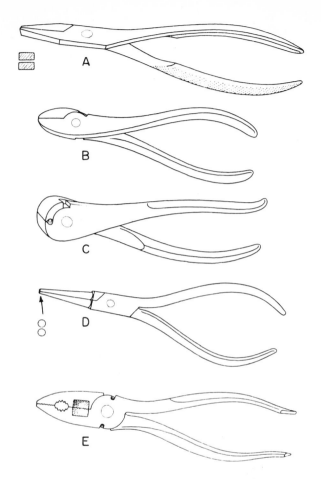

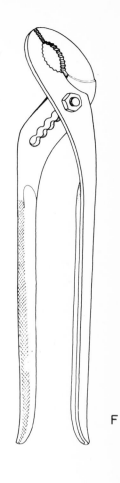

F

Pliers: A. Flat nose; B. Diagonal cut; C. End nippers or jewelers' cutters; D. Round nose; E. Combination side cutter, flat nose, and cutting-edge pliers; F. Plier-wrench (utility or arc-joint pliers). B and C are normally used for cutting wire, etc., A is used for turning eyelets and soft curves in wire, E and F can be used to bend, cut, and hold cylindrical objects.

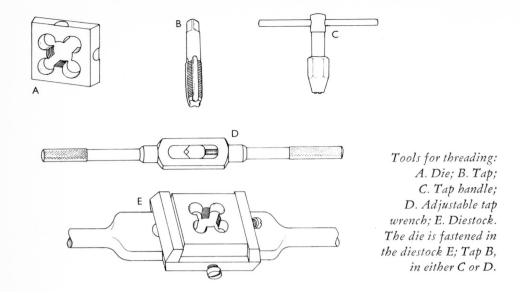

*Tools for threading:
A. Die; B. Tap;
C. Tap handle;
D. Adjustable tap
wrench; E. Diestock.
The die is fastened in
the diestock E; Tap B,
in either C or D.*

Materials

Metalworking depends on the ability to shape and prepare refined metals. Early in the history of man, only three pure metals were known—gold, silver, and copper. Iron was discovered much later and it became the most meaningful metal for mankind.

It was soon discovered that two or more known metals could be combined (alloyed) to form a completely new metal with different properties and appearance. *Bronze* was the earliest alloy discovered, made by combining copper and tin. Still later, man discovered how to alloy copper with zinc to get *brass,* which slightly resembles bronze.

For a time, metalsmiths were very engrossed with trying various methods of alloying copper, zinc, and nickel. The new alloy they developed was called German silver, or nickel silver, although it had no silver content. *Stainless steel* was discovered about the time of World War I and it was given the misnomer of rust-free steel; although corrosion-free steel would be a more accurate term. Stainless steel is an alloy of iron, chromium, and nickel. This iron alloy created a real revolution in the manufacture of everyday utensils. In industry, lightweight aluminum alloys brought about a great revolution in the construction of machinery. Aluminum can be alloyed with a combination of magnesium, copper, and manganese to produce *duralumin;* with copper alone, or with silicon.

The following section will discuss some of the metals that are practical working materials for the amateur metalworker.

Silver and Gold

These pure, precious metals do not oxidize (combine with oxygen) when heated in the open air.

Silver (Argentum, Ag) is very soft and therefore seldom used in its pure state. Usually it is alloyed with larger or smaller amounts of copper but never more than 17% so that the alloy always contains at least 83% pure silver. Adding copper is necessary to give greater hardness since pure silver is too soft to work with. Sterling silver must contain 925 parts of pure silver to 1000 parts of alloy, and other silver alloys contain 800-900 parts of pure silver to 1000.

Silver is a soft, white, ductile and easily worked malleable metal that does not oxidize but slowly becomes darker as it combines with volatile chemicals in the air. It can be chased (engraved), rolled, and stretched, without snapping or cracking. If it is to be forged it must be annealed. Soldering on silver can only be done with silver (or hard) solder which has a silver content of at least 48%—50%.

Gold (Aurum, Au) is not usually used for hobby work since it is so expensive. It is a soft yellow metal with a bright lustre and remains unchanged in the air. It is the toughest and yet most easily forged of all metals.

Gold's purity is universally measured by its weight in Carats which usually appears on any article made of gold.

24 Carats—pure gold
18 Carats—18/24 pure gold with 6/24 metal alloy
14 Carats—14/24 pure gold with 10/24 metal alloy
 8 Carats— 8/24 pure gold with 16/24 metal alloy

Some countries, such as Switzerland, do not consider 8 Carats as real gold.

Copper (Cuprum, Cu)

Copper was the earliest metal known and used (about 4000 B.C.) It is an attractive, soft metal well-suited for hobby work. It is soft and easy to cut and work, although at the same time it is strong enough to keep its form. It can be forged at a relatively low temperature, 1292° F. The color is beautiful whether the metal is highly polished or has tarnished.

In former days pots, kettles, and other kitchen utensils were made of copper, but these beautiful antique articles have been almost completely displaced by the more practical mass produced kitchenware of aluminum or stainless steel. Old coppersmiths were fine artists and prominent craftsmen. Many of their products can be seen today as prized collector's items in the home to delight the eye and still to be used. They remind us of a past era when the craftsman had the time to linger over his work and had the artistic urge to create objects of beauty. In recent years some crude copies have appeared on the market but they lack the old coppersmith's inherent sense for beautiful form.

If copper is exposed to damp air for quite a long time, the metal becomes coated with green copper acetate. The roofs of old churches and castles which appear to have a pretty green color are usually of copper. This verdigris coating protects the metal against deeper corrosion and it is very poisonous. Because of this peculiarity copper used for preparing food must always have a protective coating.

Hammered copper must first be annealed, as the metal will become hard and brittle as it is worked. Repeat the annealing several times if necessary.

Copper Alloys

Bronze is an alloy of copper and tin.

This alloy was so important that its name was given to an entire historical period, the Bronze Age, when the strongest weapons and tools were made of bronze. In Northern Europe the Bronze Age is estimated to have covered the period from 1700-500 B.C., which reveals how important this alloy had become.

Bronze is much harder than copper, which made it possible for Bronze Age Man to cast better weapons, axes, and other items, in this alloy. It is rather easy to cast and bronze has long been used for ship and church bells as well as commercially for machine bearings, bearing linings, etc., and for decorative items such as candlesticks and statuary.

The tin content in the alloy will vary according to the purpose for which it is designed. Cannon bronze contains 9% to 10% tin, bell bronze 20% to 25%, while coin bronze only contains 3% to 8% tin plus 1% to 10% zinc.

Brass is an alloy of copper and zinc. The copper content is given in percent and the copper alloy is identified by this. For example, if you use brass 63, the alloy will contain 63% copper.

Brass types with high copper content are called *tombac*. Tombac is redder in color than brass and is used in inexpensive jewelry.

80—pink tombac (low brass)
85—yellow tombac (red brass)
90—red tombac (commercial bronze)

When tombac is used in machine parts 2% to 3% tin is usually added.

Brass has just about all the good qualities of copper, but due to the addition of zinc the characteristic copper color disappears and is replaced by a more yellowish tinge. Brass is a bit more difficult to prepare than copper, and it will easily crack if it gets too hot or too cold.

Annealed brass is strongly attacked by oxides, and the surface should be rinsed in a bath of 3% sulphuric acid, 3% nitric acid, and 94% water. Submerge the brass object for about 8 hours, the surface can then be easily cleaned off with a steel brush. After cleaning, rinse the object thoroughly in cold water, and dry.

German Silver (Nickel Silver) is a copper alloy that may contain, for example, 55% copper, 25% zinc, and 20% nickel.

The alloy is used, among other things, for surgical instruments, drawing tools, etc. The color is yellowish-white but is generally silver-plated for greater protection against chemical attack and to disguise the often dull color of the alloy.

Alpaca is a type of nickel silver that is almost silver-white but without the noble lustre of the silver. Nickelin is a nickel silver alloy with a high nickel content (approx. 45%). Nickelin wire, because of its high heat-resistant quality, is used a great deal in electronics (resistance wire) and in ceramic firing.

Nickel silver is fairly easy to work with, but for hammering and chasing you must first anneal it and then cool it off slowly to get the material sufficiently soft.

The copper alloys mentioned above are the most important ones and have the greatest practical use. Innumerable copper alloys formed with other metals are much too large a topic to discuss here. You should know, however, that mixtures of copper and aluminum make *aluminum bronze;* copper and manganese make *manganese bronze;* copper, manganese, and zinc, make *silver bronze* (aluminum paint); and copper, zinc, and iron form *delta metal* (an English trade name for many alloys).

Aluminum (Al)

Aluminum is not found in pure form but is made by the electrolysis of aluminum oxide.

Until about 75 years ago this silver-white, extremely lightweight metal was fairly rare because of the difficulties of its extraction. Today it is second only to iron and steel as the most useful metal, and its uses increase day by day.

Aluminum, although very lightweight (a property that determines many of its uses) is not very strong and is, therefore, usually alloyed in combination with some other metal. The most important alloys are:

Aluminum-copper, which has a small percentage of copper. It is tough and resistant to chemical action but is not very strong. Increasing the copper content increases the strength but at the same time reduces the toughness.

Aluminum-zinc usually has a zinc content of 8% to 20%. Smaller parts of copper or of nickel are also added.

Aluminum-silicon may contain 87% aluminum and 13% silicon from which the term 13-alloy derives. Great strength and toughness and good resistance to chemical attack are well-known properties of 13-alloy.

Duralumin is an alloy containing several substances, usually 94% aluminum, 3.5% to 5.5% copper, .5% to .8% manganese and .5% magnesium. In several respects, including strength and hardness, duralumin has the same good qualities of some types of steel.

Electron alloy is the name of an alloy that contains 90% to 95% magnesium and 5% to 10% aluminum.

Zinc (Zn)

Zinc is a metal with a bluish surface and strong lustre. Due to the deleterious effects of air the metal is coated with a thin, protective layer which makes the zinc surface appear gray. Zinc is used as a protective cover on iron (galvanizing), for negative electrodes in voltaic cells and for various alloys. Zinc is also used for the making of chemical flux.

Tin (Stannum, Sn)

Tin is a silver-white metal which is somewhat harder than lead. It is pliable and ductile but not very strong.

In the past, practical utensils such as dishes, bowls, pitchers, etc., were made of tin, either cast or pressed in a pressure bench. Such old tinware items are very rare today and are eagerly sought by antique collectors. Tin objects may be affected after some time by a condition called "tin pest" that mars the surface of the tin by creating ugly scars and bulges.

Tin has a very low melting point and is therefore used in a tin-lead-alloy as a soldering agent (soft, or tin solder). Tin is very important for use as a cover for processed food cans (tinned sheet metal) and, of course, as a component of many alloys.

Lead (Plumbum, Pb)

Lead is a very heavy metal, but at the same time it is so soft that it can easily be rolled, pressed, and pulled into wire, pipe, and bars. Cast lead sheets were used a great deal in former times as roofing material, on rural churches, etc.

The surface of lead oxidizes rapidly in the air. Its melting point is low, about 572° F., and it is widely used, as mentioned earlier, together with tin as a component in soft solder.

Lead poisoning is very dangerous and will seriously affect those who use lead or materials containing lead, carelessly, in their work; electricians, telephone employees, printers, painters, etc. If you work with lead, avoid inhaling it or getting any in an open cut. Try to maintain complete personal cleanliness and be sure to have good ventilation in the workrooms.

White Metal
(Babbitt Metal, Anti-friction Metal)

White metal is an alloy of tin and lead with antimony, for example, 80% tin, 15% antimony, and 5% copper. When tin is combined with antimony it becomes hard, but at the same time, brittle and to make the alloy stronger small amounts of copper are added. By adding lead (usually from 3%) white metal becomes harder.

Iron (Ferrum, Fe)

Iron is the cheapest of all metals and probably the most widely used.

Pure iron is very soft and is only used for special purposes. Carbon content and various alloys are the factors which give the different types of iron widely dissimilar properties. Generally, one can say that iron containing less than 2% carbon can be forged and cast, while iron containing more than 2% carbon cannot be forged but can be cast. Soft steel (forgeable iron) contains less than .5% carbon, hard steel from .5% to 1.6% carbon, and cast iron contains about 2.3% carbon.

By warming iron to a sufficiently high temperature, it can be forged, bent, stretched, and shaped.

For tools and the like use steel alloyed with chromium, vanadium, or other metals. H.S. steel (high-speed) which is used especially for drills, hacksaw blades, chisels, etc., is alloyed with wolfram, chromium, and vanadium and is excellent for its long-wearing and cutting ability.

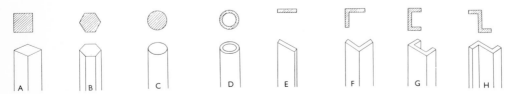

Profiles and shapes of stock metal supplies: A. Squared bar; B. Hexagonal bar; C. Round bar; D. Tube or pipe; E. Flat iron and brass; F. Angle iron; G. U-profile; H. Z-profile.

Materials - Sizes and Shapes

When using one or another type of metal, you begin with the raw material which is worked until the piece assumes the desired appearance and shape. Both experts and amateurs must use this process which simply is the only one possible and has been the basis for all handwork since antiquity.

The process does, however, require a sense of proportion for the piece to be used in making the project. For example, if you planned to make a toothpick you would not select a large tree as raw material.

A toothpick does not have much to do with metalworking, but the example simply illustrates that you must choose your raw material sensibly.

Machine shops try to select pieces of raw materials for each project which will require the least work. They do this to avoid expensive waste of material, and to conserve the cost of running the machine.

For the amateur, conditions are slightly different, as he will work for pleasure for many hours. But similar to the craftsman's problems, the smallest piece of metal must be paid for, and any waste costs money, which can make a simple project quite expensive.

One must try to find some raw material which resembles the finished article as closely as possible in shape and appearance. The first steps should be done completely by clipping, cutting, and bending, rather than by time-consuming filing. Take advantage of the many pre-processed metals available.

Most metals are available in *sheet metal* (very thin sheets), *sheets, solid bars* (round, square, and hexagonal), *tubes, wire,* and other *shapes.* Each of these comes in various dimensions from very small to extremely large.

Metal is usually sold in whole lengths, and in most cases is too large for hobby use. But some large hobby and crafts suppliers will sell smaller pieces so you can get exactly the length or segment you need and the price is then a bit higher.

The drawings on p. 22 show some of the available shapes and profiles of metal pieces.

You can also get rectangular and grooved brass tubing, wire in many thicknesses, *foil* (thin, pliable sheets), and sheets.

Joining Methods

Different methods are used in joining metals; some form permanent joints, while others form detachable joints. In every case you must choose the method that you feel is best for your project.

Welding requires great skill and expensive equipment, thus most hobbyists will use solder, rivets, or screws for joining.

Soldered and riveted joints are permanent; they cannot be loosened without heat. Screw connections, on the other hand, are easily taken apart with a screwdriver or wrench.

Soft Soldering

There are two types of soldering: soft soldering and hard, or silver soldering.

Soft or sweat soldering is easy to do at very low temperatures, but the finished joint cannot tolerate hard, mechanical strain. Hard soldering is done at relatively high temperatures, and it forms a more solid and durable joint.

Soft soldering is so easy to do that anyone can learn to solder correctly after a few attempts. Hard soldering, however, is more difficult to learn, and requires special equipment. Two pieces of metal "glued" together with melted solder will bond together when the solder cools and hardens just as two glued pieces of paper will. You can solder most metals in this easy way except aluminum, which will need special soldering agents.

The most important soft soldering tool is the soldering iron. You can use a small, inexpensive soldering iron to be warmed over an open flame (Bunsen burner), or an electric soldering iron which is faster and easier to work with. For small pieces use a soft solder wire which comes in small amounts. This wire often has a core containing the soldering agent or flux, rosin, or pine resin. You can also use a flux that is bought ready to use for metalworking or one made with hydrochloric acid, in which small pieces of zinc are dissolved. When the acid stops bubbling you know you have added enough zinc. Filter the liquid. (Be careful not to burn fingers and clothing!) Besides the soldering irons, solder, and fluxes, you will also need a needle file and a piece of sandpaper for cleaning the soldering iron.

If the point, the chisel-shaped edge, of the soldering iron has tarnished black, it must be cleaned quickly and effectively with a file. In mild cases a piece of sandpaper will suffice. Clean the point until the shiny copper appears. Do not warm the soldering iron until it is completely clean. During the warming, try holding a piece of solder against the tip of the soldering iron now and then. When the solder melts rub it over the point. The melted solder should spread evenly over the entire surface of the iron's edge. If there is a place where the solder will not stick, try dipping the point in flux and try again. Usually, however, the solder runs easily and covers the point with a shiny, silvery layer. Clean off the excess solder, with an old cloth and the soldering iron is ready to use again. It is "tinned." Without this preliminary tinning, it is useless to try and solder.

Small articles are most easily soldered by holding the point of the soldering iron against the metal until it is thoroughly warmed. Then cover the area to be soldered with flux, and hold a piece of soft solder wire against it, close to the hot iron. The soft solder will melt and distribute itself along the joint to be soldered. Larger pieces can be pre-warmed over a Bunsen burner, and the solder can be applied with the soldering iron, letting its warm tip catch a few drops of solder. Here, too, the area may be covered with flux and the soldering iron brought along the joint in a gentle and regular tempo, pulling a thin strip of soft solder behind it.

Why do so many soft solder joints fail?

There are two things you must watch carefully on every soldering job:

1) Completely clean the area to be soldered.

2) Warm the soldering iron sufficiently.

If the soldering iron is not warm enough, the solder will harden with a dull and gritty surface, and this type of soldering is not any good. To solder correctly, the solder must harden evenly and have a glossy surface like newly polished silver. The entire area should be covered with a very thin layer of solder, using as little as possible! This makes the finest and most durable joint.

If the area is not really clean, the solder won't "bite" and in some places every attempt to get the solder to stick will fail. Should this occur there is only one thing to do—start over again with a thorough sanding and cleaning, even using a file.

After cleaning, the area to be soldered must

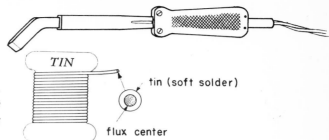

An electric soldering iron. Detail drawing shows the soft solder with a flux core.

TIN

tin (soft solder)

flux center

be carefully brushed with flux. This is done to remove the inevitable oxide film that forms on all shiny metal surfaces and which will hinder soldering. In warming, the piece oxidizes, and it may be necessary to apply a little extra flux while soldering. But no matter how much flux is used it won't cancel out the initial cleaning. Both processes are necessary.

Soft solder usually consists of an alloy of equal parts of tin and lead with a melting point of about 482° F. If the proportion of tin and lead is changed, the melting point also changes. An alloy with 64.5% tin and 35.5% lead will have a melting point of about 365° F. While making the alloy a small percentage of antimony is added to the tin and lead alloy. For special jobs there are other combinations with melting points lower than the boiling point of water. (Consult your dealer for available brands.)

As soon as the warm soldering iron is removed, the soft solder will dry in a few seconds, and the piece must be kept absolutely still!

Hard Soldering

While every amateur can learn to make good soft solder joints, he will find it is much more difficult to use hard solder. Not because it is a more involved or difficult soldering process in itself, but because it is generally a matter

Soft soldering with a comparatively large soldering iron of the type that is warmed over an open flame. The piece is held firmly with the round-nose pliers. Sticks of soft solder are seen at the top.

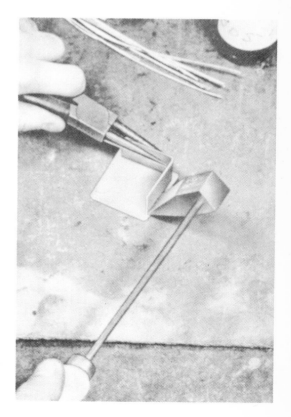

25

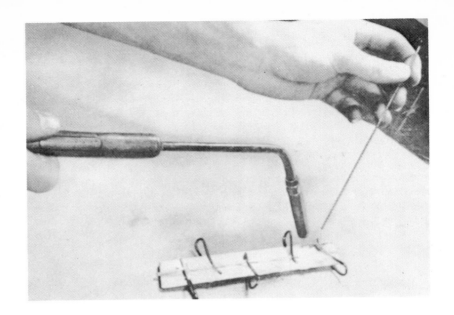

Hard soldering with a gas torch. Hold nozzle handle in the right hand. The metal to be joined is held together with clips. Soldering is done on a fireproof surface such as sheet asbestos.

of experience to judge the temperature correctly and this can only be learned by making *many* tests on scrap metal. For hard soldering you must have a soldering *torch* (propane), preferably the type which has a nozzle that can be adjusted for different size flame points, larger or smaller, and driven by high pressure.

A torch run by gas or petroleum *can* be used for soldering, but it is time-consuming to warm it up and light it, awkward to use, and runs some risk of exploding if it is pumped too hard in an attempt to get extra heat.

Hard soldered projects are heated directly by the gas flame from the burner, so it is impossible to hold them in place with tongs, etc. Position the pieces accurately, and fasten them with binding wire or small clips. For thin sheets, etc., you can use cotter pins which are normally used for securing bolts in an automobile. A cotter pin is shaped much like a hairpin and has two legs which will hold the metal in position.

Just as in soft soldering, all grease and dirt must be removed and the area must be kept clean. You must also use a flux to cover oxidation on the metal surface. Borax mixed with distilled water may be used or you can buy one of the various hard solder fluxes. Mix the flux to a soft paste before it is put on the area to be soldered.

Both fluxes and solders can be purchased in hobby craft or art supply stores. Be sure to get solders which do not require too high a temperature so you can work more easily with them.

Clean a ⅛″ strip along the edges of the surfaces to be soldered. Apply the flux to the cleaned edges on both pieces and bind them together with binding wire or hold them in place with cotter pins or clips. A little extra flux can then be applied.

Place the piece on a *heat proof surface* such as an asbestos pad, charcoal soldering block, or a stack of bricks.

Bring the hard solder (which may be in

wire form) and the dry flux together at the top of the piece. Light the gas burner and adjust it for a large, somewhat fan-shaped flame.

Aim the flame toward the soldering area, and move it backward and forward to insure an even distribution of heat. If one piece is thicker than the other, concentrate most of the heat on the thicker piece.

After the flame has been applied to the piece for some time the flux will begin to bubble, but soon it will form a layer over the soldering area. Continue heating until the piece becomes reddish-brown. At this point the flux has the appearance of melted glass.

Now shift the gas torch to the left hand. Hold the stick of solder in your right hand with one end on the soldering joint, but do not hold the solder directly in the flame. The solder will get its warmth from the metal itself.

Dip the warmed end of the stick of solder into the dry flux, which will adhere without difficulty. Hold the stick against the joint again and continue heating. The flame, however, must not touch the solder directly.

At a certain point the solder begins to melt and runs down into the joint. If it does not flow freely, add more flux with an old tea-spoon or a flat piece of iron.

When the joint is well-filled with solder remove the flame and solder stick.

Now the piece is red-hot. After a short cooling off period, if it is of steel or copper, you can dip it in water to cool it quickly. Brass articles must always have time to cool off slowly and should not be dipped in water.

After cooling, remove the binding wire, clips, or cotter pins and scrub off the rest of the flux in warm water.

The process described here generally covers the method used for hard soldering. Difficul-

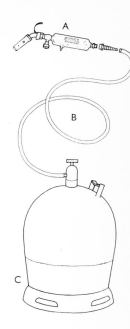

Hard soldering equipment: A. Flame nozzle with handle (notice the hole for air intake, shut off valve—next to the handle— and the gas outlet); B. High pressure hose; C. Gas tank.

ties arise in judging the correct time for adding the solder, but this is a skill that can only be acquired with experience, by trial and error. As a clue, carefully notice the color of the warmed piece and the appearance of the flux. You must add the solder at just the correct moment if the soldering is to succeed.

Riveting

The art of riveting metal pieces together has been practiced for thousands of years, and in spite of newer methods such as welding, riveting is still employed today. A riveted joint is very durable, and it is quick to make, but on the other hand, it can only be taken apart by breaking the rivet.

Larger rivets are warmed to red-hot before they are flattened out. Smaller rivets can be inserted cold.

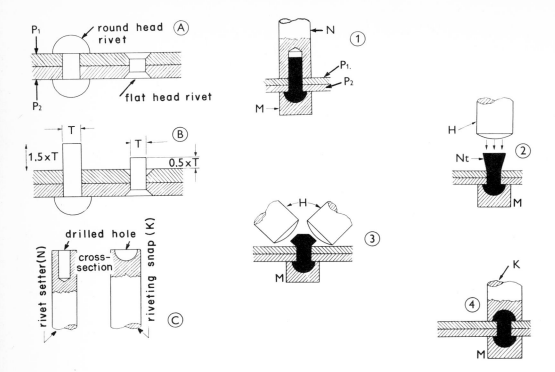

The two most important types of rivets are shown in drawing A. On the left is a round head rivet, at the right is a flat head rivet. The two rivets join plates P1 and P2, shown in cross-section.

A well-made rivet joint should be identical on both sides of the joint. The original rivet head is on one side but you will have to make a matching head on the other side—this takes talent!

In order to make the lower rivet head, of course, you will have to allow some extra length for it.

You will have to determine the extra rivet length needed according to the size of the pieces you are riveting together. Buy the rivets long enough, then cut them off in suitable lengths. This must be done in advance.

Drawing B shows how to compute the excess length for the rivet. If the rivet has a round head (left), figure the extra piece as $1\frac{1}{2} \times T$, with T the diameter of the rivet. For one with a flat head, figure the extra rivet piece as only $\frac{1}{2} \times T$.

If the riveting is to hold and look well, you cannot simply place the rivet in the drilled-out hole and hammer away at the protruding end until the pieces more or less fit together. You must make careful preparation!

To *countersink* rivets, use rivets with flat heads, and drill a hole through the pieces using a drill bit with a diameter which corresponds exactly to the diameter of the rivet. Then countersink the hole on both sides, placing and adjusting the rivet in the hole so that the proper amount of extra length appears on the other side. It is important that the rivet be pressed in tightly. Use a rivet setter (a type of mandrel) with a depression that corresponds to the rivet. This tool is shown in cross-section in drawing C, on the left.

Place the head of the rivet on an anvil, and, supporting the piece as well as you can, position the rivet setter and set the rivet with several strong hammer blows. This will force the rivet completely down into the hole, and when the rivet setter is removed, you can then hammer the excess end into the countersunk hole. Ideally, you want to get the countersunk rivet exactly level with the surface of the metal. If there is still a bump at the rivet this must be smoothed off with a file. If the work has been properly done this step should not be necessary.

Countersunk rivets are easy and quick to make. If you want the rivet head to show above the surface of the metal use a round-head rivet. This process is more difficult.

To position round-head rivets, in addition to the rivet setter you should also use a *riveting snap*. This is also a type of mandrel with a small, dome-shaped depression which fits the rivet head—shown in drawing C (right). You should also use a small iron block with a hole to fit the rivet head. It will act as a support for the original rivet head when you are working and will keep the rivet head from being flattened.

Drawing 1 shows the adjusted rivet pushed through a hole in two sheets, P 1 and P 2. The round-head rivet is placed in the support block M, which is positioned on the anvil or fastened in a vise. The rivet setter, N, is placed over the rivet. Strike the rivet setter with several hard hammer blows and this will force the sheets tightly together and also force the rivet in tightly.

Drawing 2 shows the rivet setter removed. With a hammer, H, hit the rivet with heavy vertical blows so that it begins to broaden.

In drawing 3, the shaping of the rivet is continued with angled hammer blows from all sides.

In drawing 4, the last phase is shown. This is the final rounding off of the rivet. For this, use the mandrel K, and pound it with the hammer until the rivet assumes the proper shape. If the excess has also been figured correctly, the rivet should now be identical on both sides, and you should not be able to tell the difference between the original rivet head and the one you have just made.

The rivet setter and the mandrel are sometimes combined in one tool.

Soft steel rivets are most frequently used but copper and aluminum, as well as various special rivets such as tube rivets and split rivets, are also available and better than solid rivets for some jobs. You can also make rivets of wire.

Screw Joints

The screw joint is probably the most common joining method used today. As explained previously, you can cut threads in drilled holes and on cylindrical metal rods. But normally, screw joints will be made with ready-made screws and fittings.

Screw joints are used especially when you want one that can be made and loosened again, easily and quickly, if necessary.

The most important pieces for screw joints are *machine screws, bolts,* and *nuts.* Screws and bolts have an outer thread, nuts have an inner thread.

Screws come in all sizes: small and large, thick and thin, short and long, and it is always possible to find a screw to fit the work.

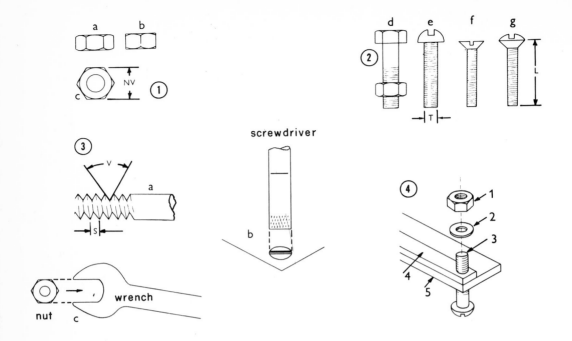

Drawing 1 (above) shows (a, b, and c) a common hexagonal nut. The outer measure NV, indicates the wrench size to loosen or tighten the nut. These nut sizes are standardized, and there is a corresponding wrench size for each. Adjustable wrenches will fit all sizes.

Drawing 2 d shows a machine bolt with a hexagonal head and nut; e, a machine screw with a round head; f, a machine screw with a flat (countersunk) head; and g, a machine screw with an oval head.

The length of machine screws (L) and the thickness (T) is figured and measured as in drawing 2. Screw measurements are given as length (in inches) x thickness (gauge).

The difference between machine metal or wood screws lies mainly in the thread angle V, and the pitch S, of the threads (drawing 3 a). Metal screws have a wider V.

The screwdrivers used for machine screws must exactly fit the notch in the head of the screw or it will inevitably slip in the notch and you may ruin the screw or the screwdriver (drawing 3 b).

If two thin sheets are to be screwed together (drawing 4), the screw 3, is inserted in sheets 4 and 5, and a washer 2, is placed between nut 1, and the material. This distributes the pressure to protect soft materials against marks.

Machine screws and nuts are made of iron and brass. Bolts, as a rule, are made only of iron or hardened steel.

Surface Treatment

Polished metals have a very attractive surface, and no further treatment is necessary. If you wish to make elaborately decorated metalwork the surface may be etched, colored, or chased.

Polishing

Metals are usually polished with *emery cloth* or *emery paper,* which comes in several grades of coarseness. Begin with a rougher emery cloth, continue with medium fine, and end with fine emery cloth. If a plain, flat surface is to be polished wrap the paper around a smooth wooden block with right angled corners, then begin. If there are curved and bent surfaces on the piece, find a pointed piece of wood so you can easily follow the intricacies in the shape of the metal, and wrap the emery paper around this. To begin, you can polish in several directions so you can clearly see any surface scratches. Later, polishing strokes must be only in one direction, lengthwise.

The treatment with emery cloth can be followed by applying fine steel wool. After using the steel wool, however, the metal surface gets dull but will have such a handsome appearance that you will probably want to leave it this way.

Metal can also be polished with pumice. You can use a cake of pumice dipped in water, or apply pumice powder with a cloth.

For finer polishing you may use Tripoli, Paris whiting, and as a final treatment, dissolved chalk.

For renewed gloss or a final polish use one of the gentle, commercial metal polishes on the market especially made for articles of brass, copper, aluminum, or silver.

Cleaning

Worked metal articles of copper or brass will become discolored (oxidized), and they must be cleaned before being polished, in a bath of sulphuric acid and water in the ratio of 1 (acid) to 10 (water). *CAUTION: This acid solution is actually weak,* but is dangerous if prepared incorrectly. *Never* pour water *into* concentrated sulphuric acid. If you do, the water will immediately turn to steam and spray the acid everywhere. *Proper method:* Water should be measured into an acid resistant container—porcelain, glass or plastic—then add the *acid* in a *very thin stream.* Remember: *acid into water,* never the opposite.

As sulphuric acid will attack the skin, use a wooden clothespin which makes a good pair of tongs to remove objects from the bath.

Submerge the metal object in the acid bath until you can see that the oxidized layer has been removed and the piece is clean. Then carefully rinse it off under the cold water faucet, and dry it thoroughly with an old cloth.

Silver objects can be treated in a similar solution, but here the acid bath must be brought to a boil, and the article is then boiled in it for 5 to 10 minutes. Remove the metal carefully and rinse thoroughly with cold water then dry it off with a lintless cloth. It is that little bit of copper in silver which is attacked by this acid treatment, and the silver will then become very white. This treatment may be repeated.

Etching

It is not very difficult to etch metal, especially copper and brass. In general, you simply draw the design on the metal surface with a *resist varnish.* The piece is then placed in a nitric acid bath which does the work. The acid actually "mills" the metal away in any places not covered with resist. When the varnish is removed the design will stand out raised in relief, and the etched background will be the lower surface.

Before you begin etching, the metal object has to be completely finished so there is no cutting, filing, or hammering to do later. And it should already have been polished and finished with steel-wool.

Metal articles must be cleaned before etching. Use a wet cloth dipped in *pumice powder, benzine,* or *turpentine.* When the piece of metal is clean, try to avoid touching the surfaces that are to be treated, since even a fingerprint will leave a grease spot which can ruin the etching.

The drawing may be made directly on the metal surface with a soft black pencil, or it may be transferred to the metal with carbon paper. Using a small watercolor brush, do the drawing with the resist varnish (asphaltum dissolved in benzine). As you paint, dry off excess varnish on the brush with an old cloth, or it will very quickly become too stiff. Follow the intricate lines of the sketch. When the painting is dry you can scratch in shadow lines, etc. But this must be done quickly, within 20 minutes after the resist varnish has been applied, or it will then be too hard and brittle. Mistakes can be scratched away with a small knife. Any scratches on the remaining surface of the metal at this stage will be no tragedy, as they will disappear in the etching.

If only one side of the metal object is to be etched, cover the other side completely with resist varnish.

When the varnish has dried completely—in about an hour or two—you can begin to etch, but there is nothing to prevent your waiting a day or two, if you wish.

For the etching solution carefully use: nitric acid thinned with water in the ratio of 1 part acid to 3 parts water. But here again, you must first pour the water into a bowl (porcelain, glass, or plastic) *before* you add the acid. Photography developing pans are also useful, if they are deep enough. The object to be etched must be *completely* submerged.

The length of time the piece will remain in the acid solution depends upon how deeply you want the piece to be etched. A stay of $1\frac{1}{2}$ to 2 hours in many cases is sufficient. It is not advisable to keep the piece in the bath too long, since the acid will also attack and break down the edges of the drawing, from the sides and from below.

Rinse off the completely etched article with cold water, and dry it with a soft cloth. This resist varnish can be removed with benzine or turpentine. The raised design on the etched background must be treated with a polishing agent to improve the surface.

Thinned nitric acid can be re-used and kept in a glass flask with a tight glass or plastic stopper. An ordinary cork stopper cannot be used as it will be decomposed very quickly by the acid fumes.

In this method the drawing becomes relief while the background is etched down. The opposite, a depressed design on an untouched background, can also be done. To do this, smear the metal surface with beeswax and scratch the design through the wax layer down into the metal with a sharp steel point. The acid will only attack those places that are not covered with wax (where the lines of the design have been made).

During the etching some unpleasant and even poisonous vapors will occur. Because of this you ought to work outdoors, on a balcony or terrace. Instead of the nitric acid bath you can also use a solution of 8¾ oz. of ferric chloride in 1 quart of water. This solution is not dangerous and will not harm the skin. But, on the other hand, it takes a much longer time than etching with nitric acid, which is customarily used by the experts.

Coloring

There are so many ways of coloring metal that it would be impossible to mention them all here. We shall only describe a few easy methods which do not require many chemicals. Many books containing specific information on this topic can be found.

Copper can be colored in a bath of *sulphurated potash, ammonium chloride,* and water. Using a glass or porcelain bowl, measure .28 oz. (8 grams) of sulphurated potash, .63 oz. (18 grams) of ammonium chloride, and pour in about a quart of very hot water. Let the solution stand 15 to 30 minutes, until the sulphurated potash has dissolved completely.

The article to be colored should be submerged in the solution and stirred occasionally with a wooden stick. In just a few moments the copper article will begin to darken, and when you think it is dark enough, remove it, rinse carefully in cold water, and dry it just as carefully with a soft cloth.

After this treatment the metal will look rather black and ugly, but used properly, fine steel wool will bring out the highlights and emphasize the shadows.

Colored copper articles should be lacquered (see below).

Brass can be colored black, but you need not color the entire surface, since you can cover it with resist varnish as was done in etching. Clean the piece with *benzine* or *turpentine* to remove any grease. Paint the design with resist varnish and submerge the article in the etching solution, mentioned above, for 5 or 10 minutes. Rinse it thoroughly in cold water then place it in the color bath solution.

Prepare the color bath with 1¾ oz. of *pure copper carbonate* and about a quart of Spirits of Ammonia.

Do not allow much time to elapse between the etching bath and the color bath. The article should be taken out of the etching bath, rinsed off, and put into the color bath as quickly as possible. A period of 5 to 25 minutes in the color bath is usually sufficient. Remove the resist varnish with benzine or turpentine.

Polish the colored brass objects with metal polishing cream. There is no need to use lacquer.

Tin can be oxidized with a solution of 3½ oz. of ferric chloride in 3⅕ oz. of water, brushed on the metal. When the liquid has dried, polish off the excess oxidation.

Thinned nitric acid will give tin a gray color.

Tinning

If you want to line a copper bowl with tin, first polish the inside surface with sandpaper and steel wool. Then brush it with flux, and position the bowl over a rather low flame (Bunsen burner or torch). Place small pieces of tin in the bowl, and when these begin to melt, move the bowl so that the tin is evenly distributed over the area.

At the end lift the bowl away from the fire and finish by evenly distributing the tin with a cloth.

If the bowl is to be used for household purposes, it must be tinned only with pure tin. Soldering tin contains lead which is poisonous and may flake off in food.

Smaller objects can be treated in yet another, and easier way. You can buy various soldering substances containing powdered tin. Simply smear some on the object, and then heat over a low flame. The tin will melt and run out over the surface as before. After cooling, polish with steel wool.

Lacquering

Highly polished metal objects do not keep their lustre long. Exposure to air tarnishes them, and they must be polished regularly. If you want to end this constant polishing, the metal object can be coated with a special metal lacquer.

If the lacquering is neatly done, it is difficult to notice that there is any lacquer coating. After this treatment the gloss will remain for a long time.

Colored metal objects should always be lacquered to protect the delicate color layer.

Metals can be covered with a lacquer of *nitro cellulose* in a solvent such as acetone. These lacquers and solvents are readily available in paint stores or arts and crafts stores.

The solvent may also be used as a thinner should the lacquer become too thick.

This lacquer mixture dries very quickly, and you cannot work it in with the brush as with other types of lacquer. Apply only a single coat, do not go over the same place twice while the lacquer is wet. If you do, the brush strokes will show. Use a brush with soft, long bristles.

Thoroughly clean the article which is to be lacquered (at normal room temperature to avoid a frosty effect) with an emery cloth, steel wool, and polishing agent (in the order mentioned). Before lacquering you must remove any grease with *benzine or turpentine*.

Enameling

You can enamel on many metals, but copper is the best. Silver and tombac (red brass) can also be used. In olden days enameling was a very complicated and elaborate task but today it can be done comparatively easily. It is always advisable to make several experiments on scrap pieces of the same metal as your original, in order to get some experience before you begin working on a finished piece of jewelry.

Several types of metal-enameling powder suited for hobby use are available at arts and crafts stores. All of them take well on copper.

Before you begin to enamel it is wise to make a copper object red-hot by warming it over the gas flame, and follow this by immediately plunging it into cold water. After this treatment the copper is dulled and must again be rubbed and polished.

Remove any grease from the object with *benzine or turpentine*. Mix the powdered enamel in a small bowl with a little water (preferably distilled water). Use a small watercolor brush to apply the solution to the copper object. Distribute the solution evenly over the piece in a fairly thin layer.

Now, you must be patient until the enamel is dry. Place it near a warm radiator. Any water drops which develop from condensation can be removed with a blotter.

Only when the object is completely dry, and not before, can you begin the firing. Support the piece with some binding wire shaped to fit and hold it over the gas flame, at first set it at low heat, then use a higher flame.

When the metal is red-hot, the enamel will begin to run together and it turns shiny and smooth. At this point the enameling is finished. Set the piece aside to cool on a fireproof surface; an asbestos sheet, for example.

Chasing

A mechanical embellishment of the metal surface is called chasing. Using steel dies (chasing tools), decorative patterns are pounded into the metal.

Chasing looks very easy to do, but good results are only possible after a great deal of practice on scrap metal.

A pattern die or motif is milled or engraved on the point of the chasing tool, and imprints this line, dot, arch, star, etc., on the metal. Professional metal chasers have several hundred chasing tools at their disposal, but amateurs will not need very many. Some homemade chasing patterns can be used. Even a screwdriver can be used for a short line, as can a chisel if it is not too sharp.

It is easiest to chase on copper and brass sheets which are not too thick. Underneath the metal sheet being worked, you can use a lead sheet for support. A steel sheet or even thick cardboard can also be used. The chasing tool is held with the left hand, while the right hand holds the hammer. It is important to learn to apply the hammer with just the proper amount of force. Not too hard, or the chasing tool will penetrate the metal, nor so weak that it imprints the metal too faintly. All the hammer blows should be with the same force so that the indentations will be identical. Usually one blow of the hammer is sufficient. Working on hard metal with large chasing tools, you may have to hit the tool several times to get the impression you want.

A real chasing hammer is best. Properly shaped, it sits well in your hand.

A special kind of decorating can be done with a bench hammer having a knob or ball (ball-peen hammer). The entire surface of the metal is worked with the hammer knob to get an uneven pattern of small indentations.

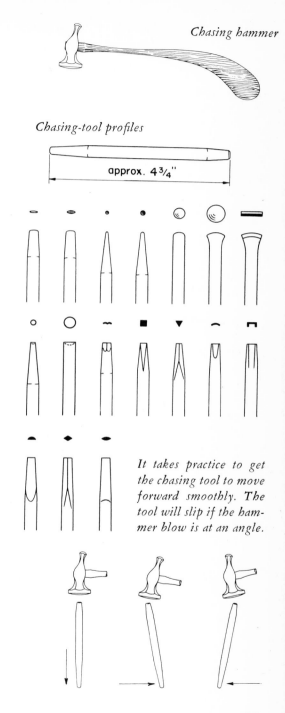

Chasing hammer

Chasing-tool profiles

approx. 4 ¾"

It takes practice to get the chasing tool to move forward smoothly. The tool will slip if the hammer blow is at an angle.

Part 2

Working Drawings and Models

EASY MODELS

Many attractive and useful objects—metal hooks, drawer handles, shelf brackets, etc.—can be made from odd bits and pieces of metal. Of course, measured in time and money, it doesn't pay to make such things yourself. But if you are really interested in metalworking, you cannot resist the thought of what you can make from a piece of metal you have found. Perhaps a decorative hinge? A drawer pull?

Although it may be a small project you can learn a great many of the practical skills and intricacies of the craft in the process. Perhaps the finished object will not be a complete success the first time, but it really does not matter. In any case you have surely *learned* something each time you finish a piece of work. Actually the most insignificant looking article requires a number of steps in cutting, marking, and bending it. When you possess these elementary skills you will not be so hesitant in considering a larger, more difficult project to do, requiring more expensive materials.

The metalworking projects in this section are small and simple. They are intended to help you begin your first work with metal.

Small Items

The drawing shows several small articles which can be made in an evening. There are shelf supports (A and B), two drawer pulls (D and E), a hanger (F), and a padlock mounting (C).

Any available material can be used, for example, strips from heavy sheets of band iron, flat iron, or flat brass. You must remember, however, that the more solid the material, the more difficult it will be to bend.

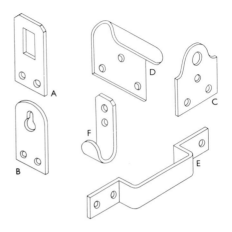

Shelf Support A. This wall mount is made from a piece of $\frac{1}{8}''$ flat iron, $1'' \times 1\frac{3}{4}''$. Drill two holes at one end with a $\frac{3}{16}''$ drill, $\frac{1}{4}''$ in from the corners. The rectangular opening near the top edge is $\frac{5}{16}'' \times \frac{5}{8}''$. Cut the hole with a chisel and smooth the edges with a file. The top corners can be cut away or filed off.

It is best to mark the metal with a real engraving tool, which has a point of hardened steel. All the measurements are transferred from the ruler to the material by using dividers.

Shelf Support B, resembles the first model except for the curved top which is drawn with a compass, and the keyhole-shaped mount.

Mark the center line carefully on the metal. Use $\frac{1}{8}''$ flat iron, size $\frac{7}{8}'' \times 1\frac{3}{4}''$. Use a compass with a $\frac{1}{2}''$ radius to mark the curve. Cut out the opening with a coping saw using a metalsawing blade and smooth the edges with a file. On the center line, make an indentation with the center punch, $\frac{1}{2}''$ from the top edge of the arch, and do the same at a distance of $\frac{5}{8}''$ from the top. Drill these two points with a metal drill bit, making a $\frac{3}{16}''$ hole at the top, and then the $\frac{5}{16}''$ hole below. Remove the walls between these holes with a chisel and smooth with a small file. This forms the "keyhole" for the nail which is to support the shelf. Drill two $\frac{3}{16}''$ holes into the shelf ends. As these shelf supports are usually used in pairs, the second one can be traced using the completed one for your pattern.

Padlock Mounting C, is made from $\frac{1}{8}''$ flat iron, $2''$ wide. Make two identical pieces.

As a radius in the two arches use $\frac{1}{4}$ of the width of the flat iron, in this case, $\frac{1}{2}''$. The topmost arch is a semi-circle, and the sides are quarter circle segments, cut with a coping saw using a metal-cutting blade.

Drill the hole for the padlock's loop with a $\frac{7}{16}''$ or $\frac{1}{2}''$ drill, and drill three holes for screws following the measurements on the drawing. These holes may be countersunk with a larger drill if you are using wood screws with flat heads. In cases where it is difficult to make the arc exactly on the metal itself, you can draw it on a piece of cardboard or heavy paper first and use that as a pattern.

Drawer Handle D, will probably be most attractive if you make it of heavy brass sheet, which is $\frac{1}{8}''$ thick.

Round the corners first with a file. You can do this "by eye," but it should be even when you finish. Fasten the piece in a vise together with a piece of long iron rod or tube (see detailed drawing). The bending is done by pounding with the hammer. Lastly, drill three holes for the wood screws. They can be countersunk with a large drill or a special countersinking bit, if you are using flat-head screws.

Drawer Handle E, is made of a piece of flat iron, $\frac{1}{8}'' \times \frac{3}{4}''$, bent into the appropriate shape. Form it on the anvil then drill four holes for wood screws.

Hook F, can be made of flat brass $\frac{1}{2}'' \times \frac{1}{8}''$. Round the hook curve over a piece of iron rod or tube, as in D.

Trim off the upper corners and round out the bottom ones with a file. Finally, drill two holes for the wood screws.

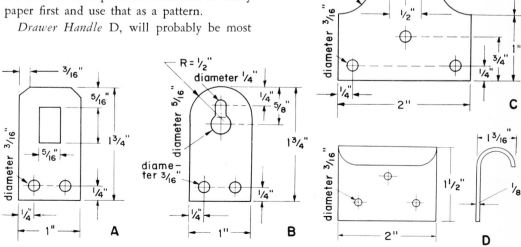

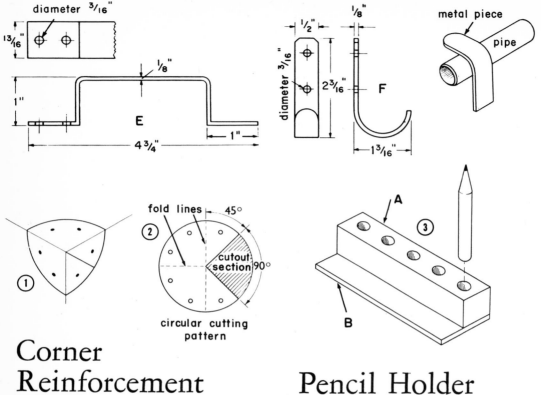

Corner Reinforcement

Pencil Holder

Drawing No. 1 shows a metal corner reinforcement for a tool box, a chest, etc. The opened cutting plan is shown in drawing No. 2. Mark a circle on a piece of sheet metal and also the lines of the 90° angle. Cut out the circle with metal shears and discard the shaded segment. Bend the piece at the dotted line so it will fit over the corner of the wooden box. The two cut edges meet on one side and can be hammered or soldered together. Small brads to hold the corner reinforcement in place can be pounded directly through the metal if it is thin enough; on heavier metal, drill holes for the screws before bending it into shape.

Drawing No. 3 shows a simple but sturdy *holder* for pencils or metal drill bits. It is made of a rectangular brass block with holes drilled all the way through. A flat brass base to prevent the holder from tipping is then soldered firmly to the brass block or fastened securely with flat-head brass screws inserted from the bottom into threaded holes $1/8''$ in diameter.

The drill holes should be made with a $5/16''$ drill bit if they are to be used for holding pencils. If they are to be used to hold drill bits, use each different size drill to drill its own receptacle.

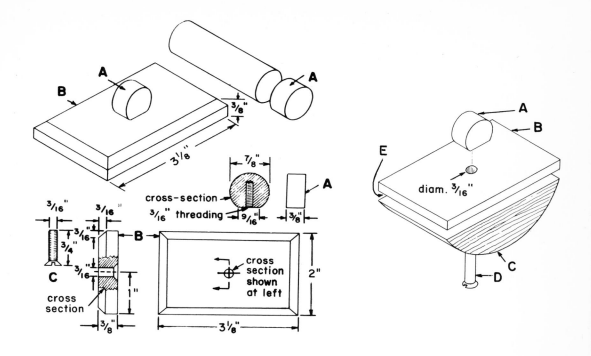

Paperweight

This attractive brass paperweight is simply ground smooth to begin. Bevel edges with a file. Drill a $\frac{3}{16}''$ hole (countersunk) in the exact center and through the plate (shown in cross-hatch on drawing). See detailed drawing B.

Cut a $\frac{3}{8}''$-thick slice from a piece of $\frac{7}{8}''$ round brass rod. Slice a segment off one side of the circle with a hacksaw to form a flat base for the piece. Then drill a $\frac{3}{16}''$ hole which is threaded with a $\frac{3}{16}''$ tap. See detailed drawing A.

Screw C, used to join the brass plate and the handle knob, has a flat head and is $\frac{3}{16}''$ in diameter and $\frac{3}{4}''$ long.

Ink Blotter

You can make this old-fashioned, "rocker type" ink blotter in much the same way as the paperweight. The measurements are given on the drawing.

The top of the blotter B, is made in the same manner as the paperweight top, but it is a little larger. Use another, wider slice of round brass rod A, for the handle. If you are able to turn a sphere with a $\frac{3}{16}''$ threading in the drilled center hole, it will make an excellent and handsome grip.

For the body of the rocker, see the measurements on the lower drawing. The brass plate and handle are connected with a flat-head screw $\frac{3}{16}''$ in diameter which is long enough to support the handle. The rocker should be made of fine hardwood.

Clamp the blotter paper between the brass plate and the rocker E. It is easily changed by slightly unscrewing the handle.

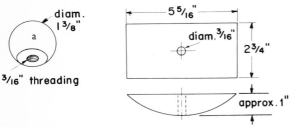

Shelf Brackets

It is quite easy to make these strong and useful shelf brackets, using $\frac{1}{8}'' \times 1''$ flat iron in the desired length.

Bend iron A into a right angle and set-in the diagonal piece which is also bent to fit closely. The diagonal part is riveted into place with flat rivets B, in countersunk holes. Drill 4 holes for screws which are used to attach the bracket to the wall and to the wood shelf.

Since you will need two brackets for each shelf—you must make another, identical set which requires careful measuring so that they match exactly. Bend both sets of brackets before you set-in the diagonal piece. It will then be easier to copy the measurements for the second bracket.

Tool Holders

The practical tool holder, Model 1, is easily made from a piece of angle iron of a suitable size. On one face of the angle iron drill a few

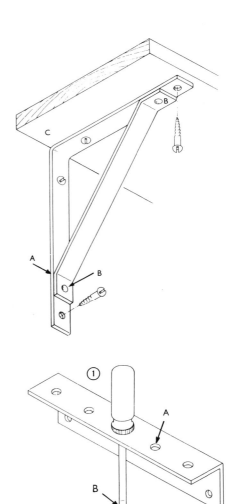

 40

holes A, with diameters to fit tools B it is to hold. On the other face, drill two or three holes for wood screws. Model 2 is deceptive as it is not as easy to make as it would at first seem. Using a thinner strip of sheet metal A, bend it over a narrow iron rod in the shape illustrated. After wood strip C, is fastened to the wall, attach the metal strip with brads D.

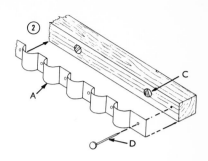

Bunsen Burner

A Bunsen burner is a very useful instrument in metalcraft. The breakdown drawing shows various parts of the gas burner. You can easily make one for yourself with the necessary extra parts obtained from an old stove. The Bunsen burner should be used only with the normal city gas supply, not with bottled gas which is dangerous.

Form the stand F, from a broad band of iron by bending it as shown. The threaded gas outlet pipe E, is mounted in the upright of the stand—to the nut—and nozzle K, is screwed to it. Immediately above the gas jet in D (black dot), drill a hole H in the stand using a $\frac{9}{16}''$ diameter drill, in which a piece of $\frac{1}{2}''$ brass tubing A, is attached above and below, with nuts B and J. The gas outlet pipe becomes the flame tube. The two nuts raise or lower the position of the flame tube until the flame burns steadily, without hissing or going out. The gas stream C, must flow up the center of the flame tube A. Drill 2 holes G, in the lower part of the stand for two screws with which to attach the stand to the worktable.

Drawing 2 shows the side detail of the burner; A is the flame tube, F the stand, and L is the gas jet beneath the flame tube.

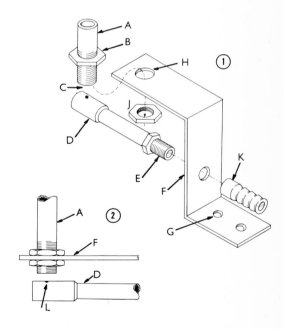

Soldering Iron

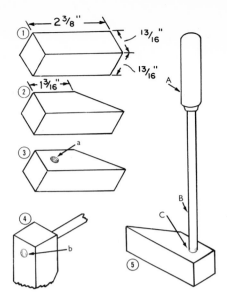

The dedicated craftsman can make a soldering iron with rectangular pieces of copper approximately $3/4''$ x $3/4''$ x $2\frac{1}{2}''$. No. 1 in the illustration is the rectangular copper piece. In No. 2, a triangular piece of copper has been cut away with a hacksaw. In No. 3, a $1/4''$ hole is drilled at A, through the copper piece. Use a $1/4''$ tap to make the threading in the hole. The shaft B, drawing 5, is made with a suitable length of solid round iron $1/4''$ thick. At one end a $1/4''$ threading C, is cut on the outer side. At the other end attach a handle A, taken from an old file. When the shaft's threaded end has been screwed into the copper piece, it is riveted as shown on drawing 4, at b.

When the soldering iron is finished, bevel the sharp edge lightly from the flat side with a file.

You must tin the soldering iron before it can be used. The lowest, cut edge is angled for easy access in soldering into deep nooks and difficult corners.

Part 3

Working Drawings and Models

MORE DIFFICULT MODELS

The models in this section are a little more difficult for the beginner to make. However, detailed descriptions and ample instructions should permit him to follow along with no trouble. The working techniques and processes which are most easily effected are used and thoroughly discussed in every project.

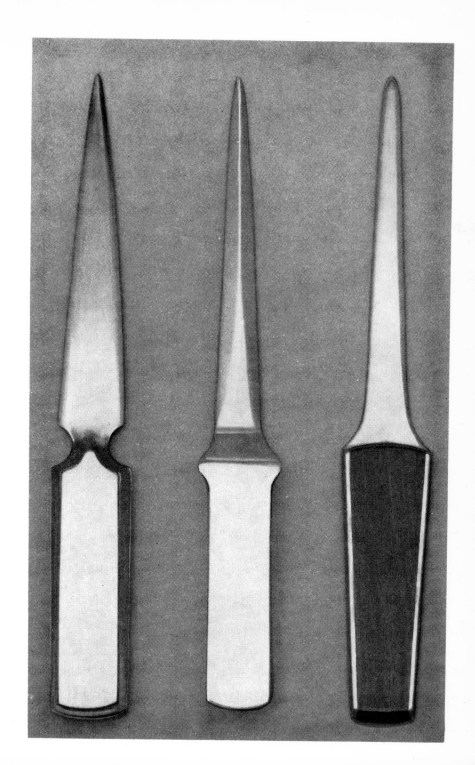

Letter Openers

None of the models shown is difficult; however, the two at the left would be preferable for beginners to construct.

The material used here is $\frac{1}{8}$" x 1" band or flat brass, but the letter openers can also be cut from sheet metal.

Draw the design on the piece and then fasten it in a vise so the top line drawn is flush with the top edge of the jaws of the vise. With hammer and chisel cut away the excess metal and then smooth the edges with a file. Using a C-clamp place the piece on a cushioning strip of wood, and again place this in the vise to hold it firm for finishing. With a rough file, shape the object into the approximate form. When the shape is close to the final design, switch to a finer cut file and smooth the edges. Lastly, remove any traces of the filing with emery cloth or paper. (See the section on Surface Treatment, p. 31.) Begin with rough emery cloth and continue polishing with progressively finer emery until the surface is satisfactory. Finish off with fine steel wool until every trace of filing marks is rubbed away and the surface is very smooth.

The center letter opener illustrated, with soldered sheet handle, is made in the same way. The two pieces are joined with ordinary soft solder. Excess solder is removed with a scraper or screwdriver. A file should never be used for this work as solder will clog the teeth of the file and it can only be removed with heat which will damage the file.

The third, and more elaborate letter opener with the wooden handle, is made a little differently. The metal edges of the handle are bent up so they can firmly hold the wedged wooden inserts. To do this, firmly fasten the piece in the vise together with a piece of flat iron. Force the edges down over the flat iron "anvil" with a hammer. Cut an ebony or other hardwood insert to fit, and glue it firmly between the prepared edges after covering the inner side with resin glue. Press the piece firmly in a C-clamp and let it stand for 6 to 8 hours. When the glue is dry, smooth down the edges of both the wooden handle and the turned up metal edges, with a file. It is not too easy to insert the wood piece as it must fit well, thus patience and painstaking work is required. If it is done well, however, the result is very attractive, the dark wood contrasting effectively with the shining metal.

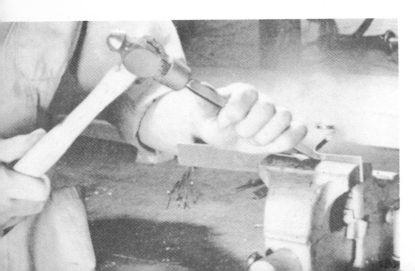

Excess material is first cut away with the chisel.

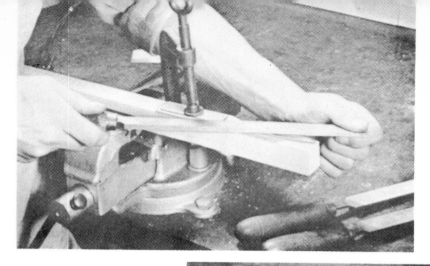

Filing with coarser, then finer-cut tools. The work is supported on a wood block held in the vise.

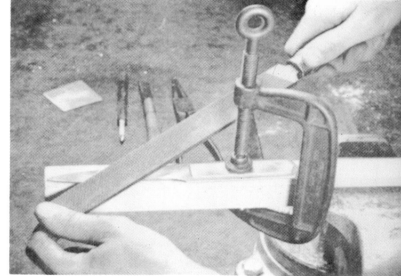

Using a finer-cut tool, file the letter opener very smooth.

Wrap emery cloth around a stick for the final grinding. 45

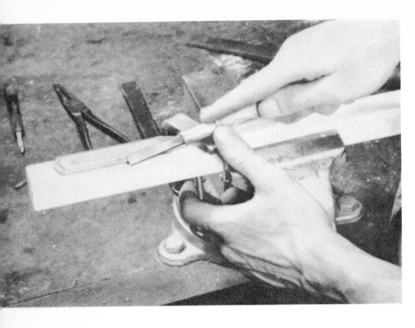

*Excess solder
is removed with
a scraper.*

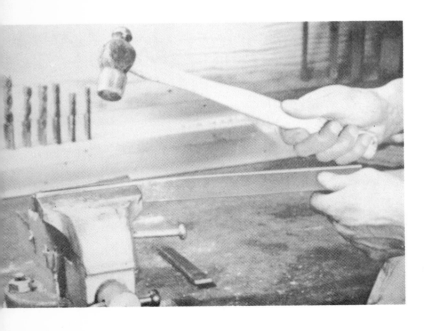

*Bend the edges
of the metal piece
over, to grip the
wood insert.*

Classic Sugar and Creamer designed by H. Winberg.

Forming and Raising Bowls and Cups

There are two common methods used to shape a bowl or cup. Low bowls are usually *formed* from the inside against a hollowed-out block of wood which fits the curve of the bowl. Deeper vases and cups are usually made from the outside by *raising* the object up—a difficult and time consuming procedure.

Forming on a wooden mold: Before you begin to cut out the metal sheet there are a few preliminary steps that must be taken. Make a good sketch of the bowl so you know exactly how the finished bowl should look. It is much easier to change the shape of the bowl on

paper, therefore it is best to continue sketching until the shape is satisfactory. When you have completed the drawing of the shape, form the mold of hardwood, no easy task in itself. Begin with a wooden block and the cutting tools you have available, and continue hollowing and gouging until the depression has achieved the correct shape.

Cut out the metal sheet a little larger than the top measure of the wooden mold and begin pounding it down into the depression. Begin at the edges, striking with the hammer in a circle toward the middle. After a short time

The bowl is shaped in a carved
wooden mold.

Exterior of bowl is smoothed with
a wooden mallet.

Final treatment with the planishing
hammer.

the metal will begin to harden and it must then be heated (annealed). It is heated to about 1292° F., and then allowed to cool. Pure copper can tolerate an immediate cooling off in cold water without harm.

After heating, continue working the piece until it fits evenly in the mold without bulging. It will, no doubt, be necessary to repeat the heating several times, but the frequency will depend upon the material and the depth of the mold.

Finally, pound the bowl with a wooden mallet over a suitable support, such as a steel ball stake. Before polishing you can also hammer the bowl with a polished planishing hammer to form a faceted surface. The hammer blows are made in a circle, and must be as close together as fish scales. The hammering must always be done on a support which fits the object in order to maintain the shape.

When the hammering is completed, file the edges smooth and then the final polishing can be done in the usual manner.

If the bowl is to have a stand, make a ring which is simply soldered firmly onto the underside. Cut a strip of metal and shape it into a ring so that the ends can be hard soldered together. If the ring is to have a conical form, or funnel shape, it can be hammered along one edge to stretch the metal. Shape the ring carefully with a file so it fits the bottom of the bowl exactly, without holes or gaps, before soldering it firmly with common soft solder.

Raising against a hard support: A great deal of patience is required for any success with this process, but do not get discouraged at the first unsuccessful attempt!

Raising is done only on the outside of the object against a hard support. In this way you actually "move" the metal in the sheet like rolling pie dough, and the thickness of the sheet becomes uneven. The support must be made of hardwood, preferably beech, and the raising hammer should be very thin. A common bench hammer cannot be used.

Holding your circle cut out of metal sheet, work it in the manner shown in the pictures on pp. 50 and 51.

Rotate the piece constantly while working it. You must practice hammering with even blows always using the same amount of force or the finished cup will lean to one side. The blows must never be so hard that the metal will crack or split. Heat the piece as soon as you notice that the material resists your work.

Continue in this manner, making small blows, until you get the generally desired form. After polishing, hammer the object smooth with a planishing hammer.

When estimating the amount of metal needed for a bowl, etc., figure the piece of metal to be 20-30% larger than the finished object. For a dish 6″ in diameter, the metal disc should measure 7⅛″ to 7½″. For vases and deep cups, double the height measure and add it to the diameter of the bottom surface. For a vase with sides 6″ high and a base of 3⅛″, the diameter of the metal sheet should be 15⅛″ (6″ + 6″ + 3⅛″).

Shaping and stretching a metal handle over the anvil horn by hammering along one edge at a time.

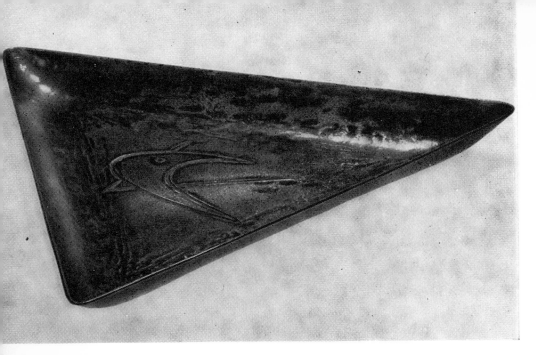

Although more difficult, hard metals can also be hammered into attractive shapes. This ashtray was hammered of flat iron.

Raising is done with a slender hammer, on the anvil.

*It takes
patience to
raise a vase.*

*A wide,
flat edge is
crimped or
fluted so that
it does not lose
its shape.*

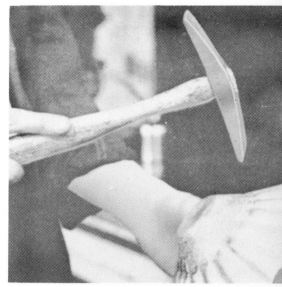

*Final
hammering
with a
planishing
hammer.*

Two bowls with simple decoration; the left is of brass, the right, of copper.
The two vases below are cut and raised from sheet copper.

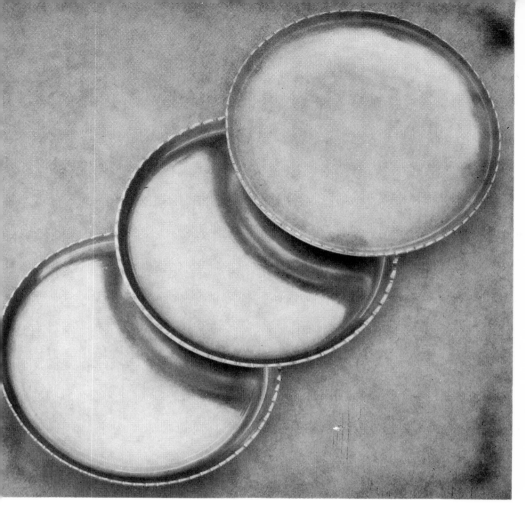

*These hammered tin coasters and modern tin dish (seen from above),
will complement your finest crystal.*

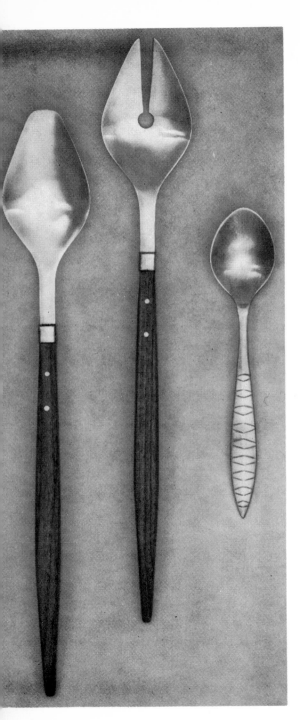

Salad Set and Serving Spoon

For these articles you will want to use silver or nickel (German) silver. Stainless steel is too hard and not suitable for hand metalworking.

The spoons in the photograph are made of sheet metal $\frac{1}{16}''$ thick. The bowl of the spoon is thinned slightly along both sides of the edges to improve the appearance.

You can chop out the wooden form for the bowl of the spoon with a chisel or saw it out following your pattern, of course, with a hacksaw fitted with a metal-cutting blade. The contoured shape is hammered in a carved wooden mold with a ball-peen hammer and is followed by planishing, as described above in raising bowls.

The shaft is made of an attractive wood and is riveted with homemade rivets of silver or aluminum wire. You must not make the rivets too tight, however, or the wood will crack.

Napkin Rings

Napkin rings and bracelets are made in the same way, and except for their size, are similar in design. Bracelet ends are not soldered together as are napkin rings.

These models are made by bending the edges, then rounding and hard soldering the ends. You can make a convex shape by hammering with a wooden mallet over a steel ball. Make a concave shape by placing it over a beveled or turned track in a piece of hard dowel (see diagrams on page 56).

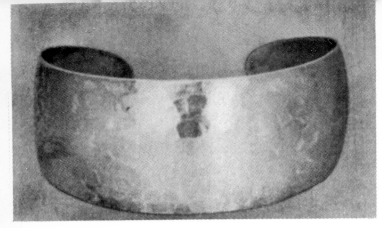

Napkin rings and bracelets are formed in a curved wooden block or over a steel ball.

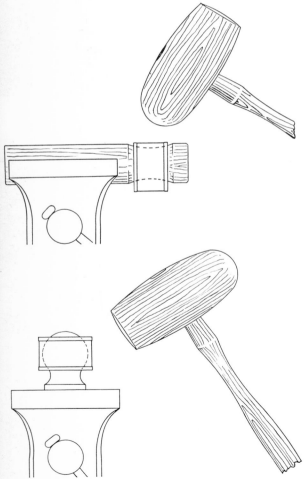

Bracelets

With a little bit of practice a talented amateur can make pretty metal bracelets. Practically all metals can be used but tin is less suitable because of its tendency to bend.

Silver, nickel silver, and copper are excellent materials for bracelets. But in craftwork it is not so much the material as the actual product that is important. As shining metal will not hide poor workmanship, try to use simple, strong designs and do them well. Work them as you did the napkin rings but finish off the ends smoothly. To decorate the surface with chasing tools, do it against a level steel plate before rounding or bending the form.

Figures can be hard soldered on the bracelet or you can inlay them, but this is a very difficult job requiring much practice. Very charming bracelets can be made with twisted wire. Use a little more than double the length of a wrist measure and bend the wire in the middle. Firmly grip the two loose ends in a vise. Insert a stick or nail through the loop and twist the wire evenly to the ends. Hammer this twisted wire flat, file the ends smooth, and hard solder them together. Try some other coiled designs in combination with flat metal shapes, soldering them to each other.

Finish and refine the shape with a wooden mallet.

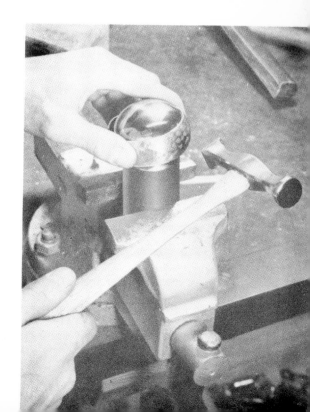

Final planishing over a steel ball.

Bracelets decorated with chasing tools. The geometric bracelet decoration is sawed, shaped, and soldered into place. The lower piece combines both types of decoration.

Decorating metal with a chasing tool. A hard metal block is used for a support to give resistance. Several chasing tools are seen in a stand.

Twisting wire held in the vise. Later, hammered flat, it makes a pretty bracelet (see page 60).

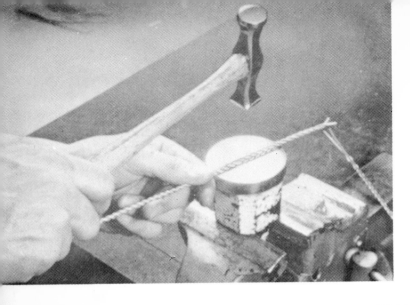

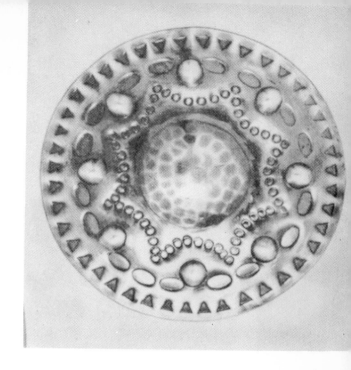

Brooches

Here again, use simple forms and patterns such as the large round ornament illustrated. It is a simple circle of silver which has been worked with a few chasing tools.

An easy way to create contrast is to color (oxidize) the completed piece and then polish only the raised surfaces.

Pin fasteners or locks are soldered firmly on the back of the ornament. All types of earring and pin backs are readily available in hobby shops.

Wood is only to be used with metal if there are bent metal edgings in the design to hold the wood piece, for you cannot glue wood to metal without some reinforcement.

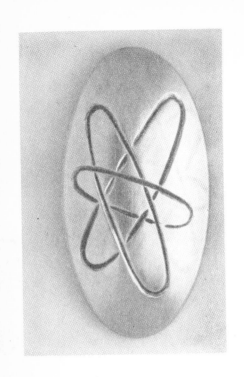

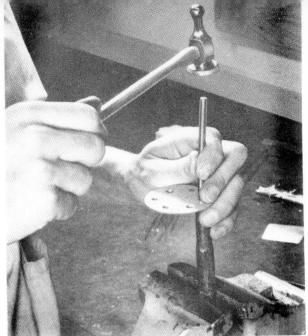

Eight circular designs made over a rivet-snap support.

Making the border pattern on a brooch.

To make a convexly-curved shape use a soft lead block as a base.

Pre-cut designs soldered to a textured brooch.

Earrings

The combination of silver and wood is very attractive but just as in the brooch, a bent metal edge must be made to hold the wood here. The metal frame is finished first and hard soldered. The wood piece is then securely inserted. If the metal frame needs an eyelet to fasten to the earring back, this must be soldered on before the wood is inserted because of the need to apply heat. Using wire, wood, and sheet metal, try creating your own unique earring designs. To make eyelets or loops, roll a long wire tightly around a knitting needle, and then cut through the entire spiral with a hacksaw.

Sawing jewelry parts from sheet metal using the coping saw.

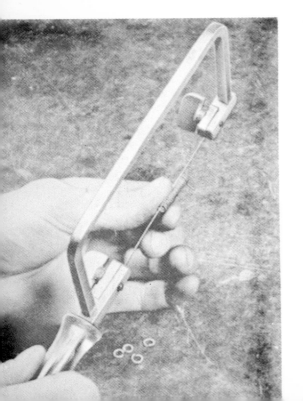

Cutting small eyelets and chain links.

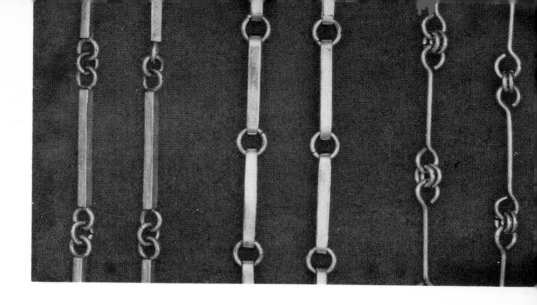

Attractive links for necklace chains or belts.

Necklaces

Chains are simple to make and large link belts are again in high fashion. The chain at the right is made of 17 gauge silver wire, and the links are held together with a double coil of silver wire.

The center chain of 18 gauge metal strips, bent together and hard soldered, is held together with rings of 12 gauge, unsoldered silver wire.

The chain at the left is much more difficult to make. The links are made of silver bars, with small eyelets soldered to each end. It requires some very tricky hard soldering to make these joints. The flame on the gas torch must not be too high and the heat is concentrated on the thickest of the pieces—the bars.

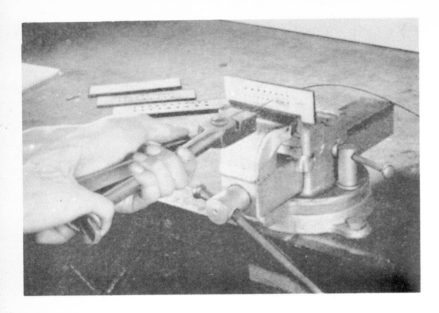

Metal wire pulled through a draw plate with strong pliers.

Pulling Wire

If you need wire of a special dimension or form (round, rectangular, or triangular) you can easily make it by using a draw plate and pliers.

Wire up to 10 gauge weight can easily be pulled by hand.

The holes in the draw plate are conical (funnel shaped), and their edges are hardened so that wires of softer metal can easily be shaped. Hard steel wire, however, cannot be pulled in the draw plate, for it will easily ruin the plate.

Metal mirror-frame with open-work decoration.

Mirror Frames

Modern mirror frames such as this, are easy projects made of $\frac{1}{32}''$, 18 gauge iron sheet. Bend the edges up into a $\frac{3}{16}''$ border, to both strengthen the frame and protect the edges of the mirror glass. The bending is easily done in a vise. Fasten the sheet between two angle irons and hit it neatly with a mallet.

Cut out the hole pattern with a chisel after marking it with a scriber. The openings, with the mirror behind them, form the decoration. Additional brass decoration can also be soldered on. The mirror is attached to the frame with small soldered strips of sheet metal.

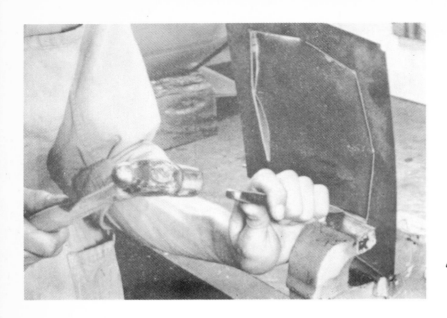

The mirror opening and decorations are cut out with a chisel.

Edges are bent over angle irons held in the vise.

Part 4

Smithing or Forging

Briefly, forging means the shaping of heated metals, particularly red-hot iron, by means of hammer blows. Naturally, this hammering is only a part of the many procedures in forging. But the hammer, anvil, and forge are the trio of tools associated with forging.

Most people know that iron and some other metals become soft when heated and thereby are easier to work. The hot metal can be bent or bowed without breaking or splitting, and can also be flattened out or thickened.

Not all metals can be forged; cast iron, for example, will turn to liquid when heated. On the other hand steel, copper, bronze, and aluminum reach a malleable plastic state in heating, and they can be forged.

Soft steels with a low carbon content are the easiest forging materials available, and furthermore, they are forgeable within a wide temperature range from 1382° to 2192° F.

The forge is fired with smithy's pea coal so that the fire will form a crust of glowing fuel. The drawing shows the construction of a stationary forging furnace. There are also transportable "field forges."

The anvil is the support for the piece being forged. Its size can vary a great deal depending on the type of work to be done. The usual forging anvil is heavy, with a surface of hardened steel. One end is shaped like a horn, and the other end can either have an extension with a rectangular hole for inserting the swages and a round hole for punches or dorns, or simply a smaller horn which usually has a flattened top.

Various hand tools are used for forging, particularly the forging hammers and tongs.

Forging hammers used as a set are a small hand hammer and a large sledge-hammer. Usually a helper swings the sledge-hammer, which weighs between 10 and 25 pounds, while the master craftsman directs the blows with the smaller, lighter hammer.

Forging tongs must be used to grasp red-hot iron as metal conducts heat. The tongs jaws are made in various shapes to firmly grasp and hold any odd-shaped object.

Various swages and chisels complete the basic equipment.

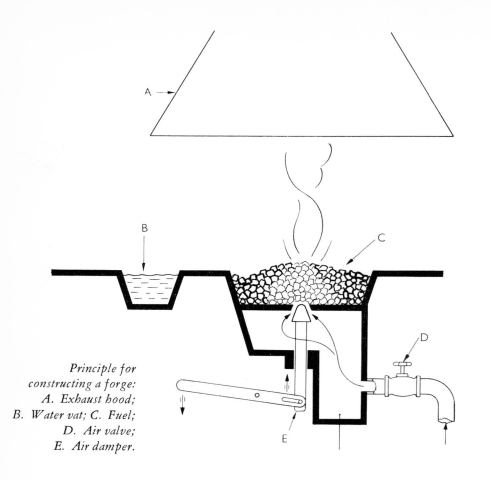

Principle for constructing a forge:
A. Exhaust hood;
B. Water vat; C. Fuel;
D. Air valve;
E. Air damper.

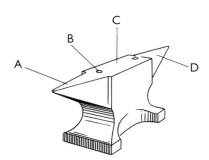

An anvil with two horns: A. Square horn; B. Swage opening; C. Surface; D. Round horn.

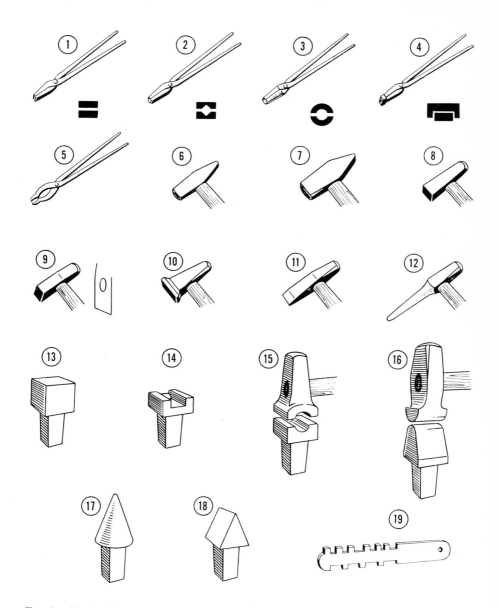

Forging Tools: Tongs—1 to 5; hammers—6 to 10; cold chisel—11; punch or dorn hammer—12; swages—13 to 16; taper pin—17; anvil chisel—18; measuring tool—19.

Forging

WORKING DRAWINGS AND MODELS

Freehand forging, where the heated object is shaped and formed with a hammer and a few tools, is the method stressed here. A completely different method is swage forging where the metal is placed between two special molds or swages of a desired shape to form your object. They are pressed or hit together around the warmed metal, which is at top heat before being positioned in the swages.

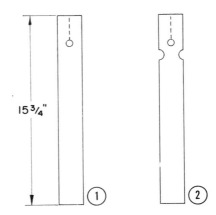

Fireplace Pokers

Flat iron $\frac{3}{16}'' \times \frac{1}{2}''$ is a good material for the fireplace poker. To get the fork-shaped points, drill a small hole about $\frac{1}{4}''$ in from the edge as seen in drawing 1. Cut the metal lengthwise with a chisel or hacksaw.

Heat the iron and with a hammer make the small notches as shown in drawing 2. Now, using the forge, work the two fork points outward, bent away from each other as shown on drawings 3 and 4. Forge the shaft to about $\frac{1}{4}''$ wide, into a square shape, drawing 5, and with a large round tongs wind the loops of the handle, as in drawing 6.

All the preceding shaping steps must be done with the metal at a red-hot condition.

If you wish to decoratively twist the shaft, fasten the object in a vise and twist it with a crescent wrench. The metal can be warmed with a gas torch for this procedure.

The photograph on p. 76 shows this fireplace poker at the left. The poker in the center is made by forging the handle. To begin, drill a $\frac{1}{8}''$ hole at a distance of about $\frac{1}{4}''$ from the edge. Chisel the iron away from the hole and toward the edge, to form the open grip. Roughly round off the corners and the remainder of the work will then consist of forging the handle smooth, working over the horn of the anvil. The handle on the third poker is made in three parts. With a chisel or hacksaw cut the flat iron into 3 parts which are well-heated, forged, then rolled for the decorative swirl with strong, round tongs.

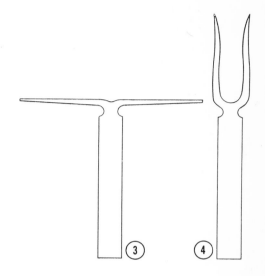

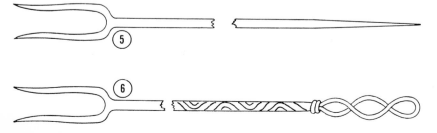

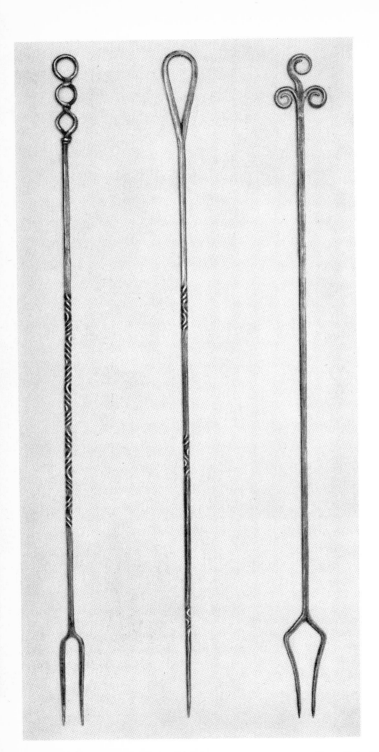

Fireplace poker and tongs.

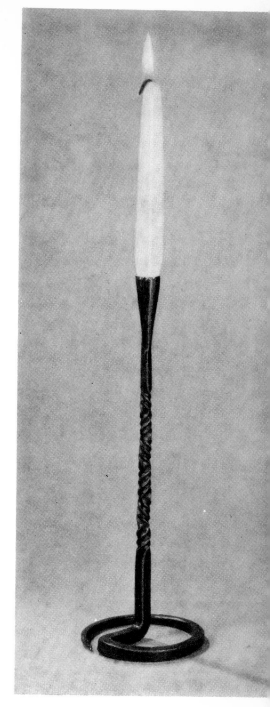

Complete candlestick made of an iron bar.

Candlestick Model 1

One end of a rod of ⅜″ square iron is widened as shown in drawing 1. This part is then forged flat, drawing 2; forced into a thin, broad plate which is rounded over the horn of the anvil, drawing 3. These edges that will hold the candle should be forced as closely together as possible as they cannot later be soldered or pounded for joining.

Forge the other end to a tapered tail, which is then bent to form an interesting, yet stable base. Before this, however, the stem of the candlestick can be decorated by twisting.

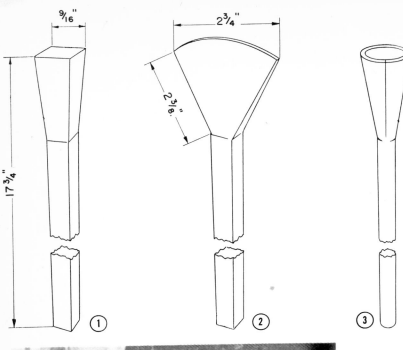

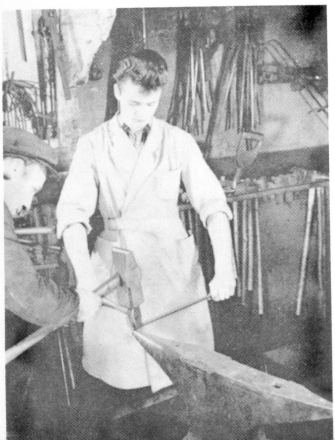

Candlestick is flattened while red-hot.

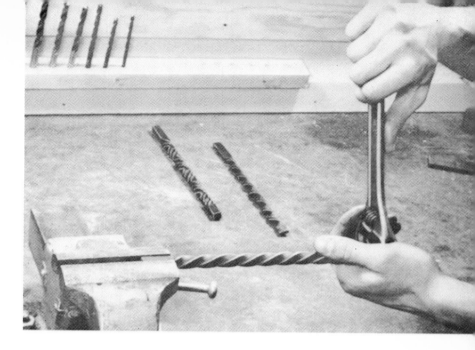

Twisting an iron bar.

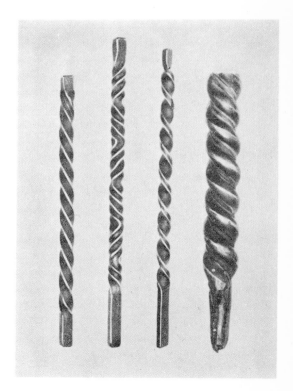

Examples of twisted iron bars.

Candlestick
Model 2

This low candlestick is made of sheet iron. The base is ⅛″ sheet, while the actual candle holder is thinner, made of ¹⁄₁₆″, 15 gauge sheet. Measure and mark the four corner sections to be cut away from the plates, then bend the base in the vise. Because of the thickness of the plate, you will need to heat it to bend it. When the object is well heated, bending is not difficult, but you may have some difficulty in bending the lines evenly. It is very important to do this correctly as the base must stand evenly so that it does not tilt the candle.

The candle cup is formed cold over a wooden mold and is attached to the base with a small scrap of pipe and a flat-head machine screw. Optional decoration on the base is made of copper and hard soldered on.

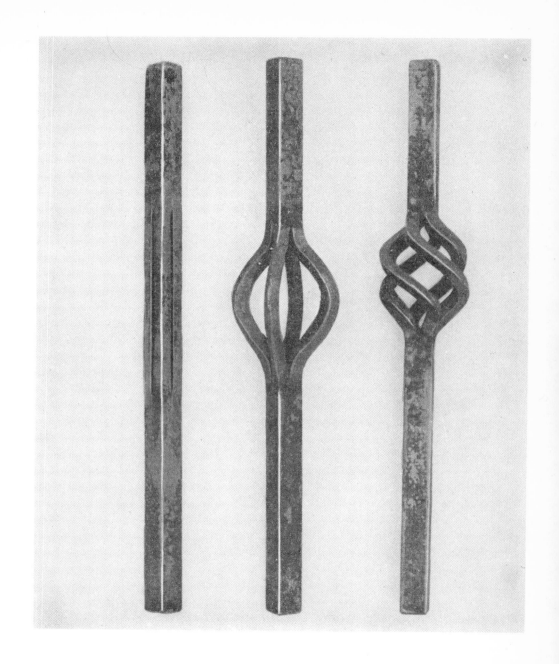

How to make slit decorations in an iron bar.

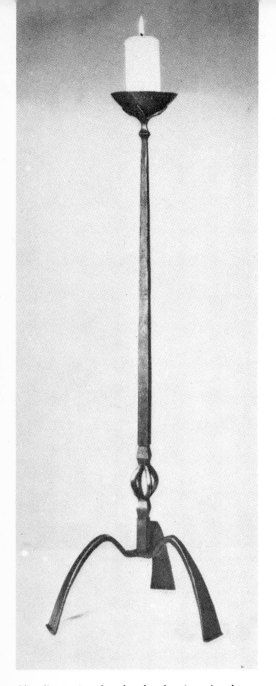

Slit decoration breaks the density of a large candelabra.

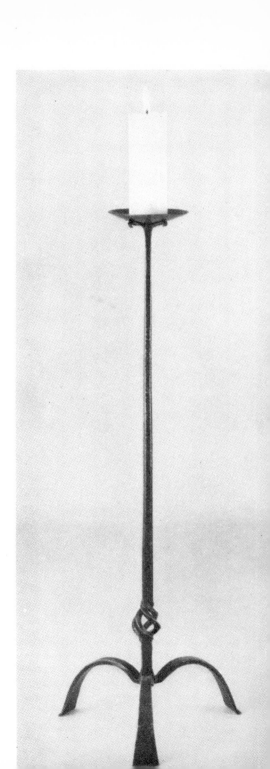

Double Candlestick

The most difficult part of making this project is in forming the tricky base. The material is 1″ round iron rod which is forced open at one end. Drill a hole with a $\frac{3}{16}$″ drill in the middle of one end, about 2$\frac{3}{4}$″ deep into the rod.

The iron is then well-heated and various conical mandrels are used in turn, first a thin one and subsequently thicker ones are forced into the hollow to widen the opening. As soon as the space is wide enough to fit over the point of the anvil horn, dispense with the mandrels and continue stretching the piece on the anvil. The small, upper part of the base is forged last. The bow-shaped iron piece which holds the candle cups is riveted in place. The candle holder itself is formed in the usual manner.

This candlestick was designed by Prof. S. Prütz, of Hanover, Germany, and is very interesting as it demonstrates how a simple iron rod can be stretched and formed at a forge.

Sconce pattern is based on an equilateral triangle.

Wall Sconce
Model 1

Despite its elaborate appearance, this beautiful sconce is forged of only one piece and it is not at all difficult to make. The material is $\frac{3}{16}'' \times 1\frac{3}{16}''$ flat iron which is cut with a chisel and twisted into shape with round tongs while red-hot. See illustration.

The candle holder section is forged exactly as the same part of Candlestick, Model 1.

Wall Sconce
Model 2

The material is $\frac{1}{32}''$, 18 gauge iron sheet. The "mirror" is a highly polished brass plate attached with two rivets soldered to the back.

Cut out the iron sheet following the pattern shown in the drawing. Bend the candle holder **and roll** the arm of the sconce, forcing it into the tube shape at the same time.

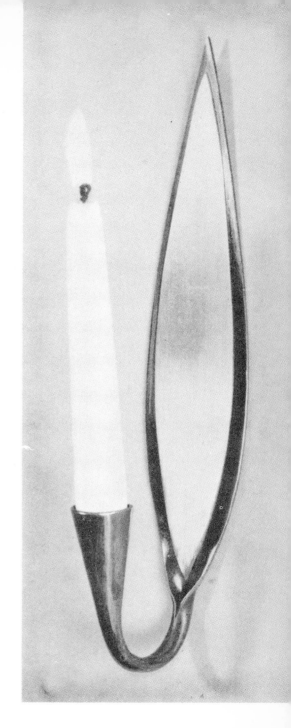

*Ends are bent
with a round-
nose pliers.*

*Forging one
of the curved
details.*

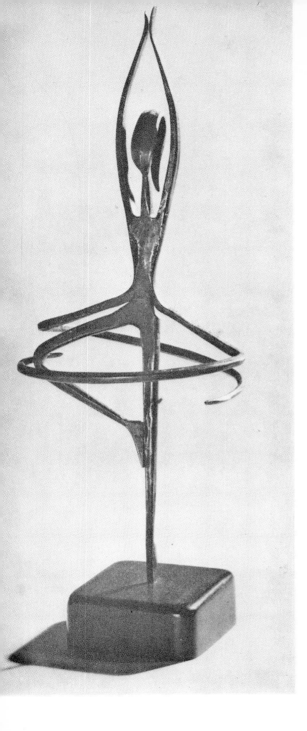

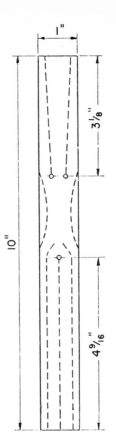

1"

3 1/8"

4 9/16"

10"

Ballerina

Why not try out your skill, making a figure? This airy ballerina is forged on the anvil, stretched and bent into shape from just one piece of metal. She stands, untiring, on a simple block.

Bootscraper Dog

This whimsical figure can be used both as a bootscraper and a doorstop. Worked on the anvil in the same method as the Wall Sconce, Model 1, it has a ring added which is held by the loop at the top.

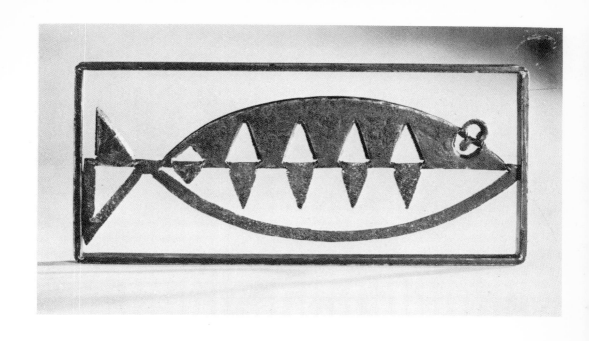

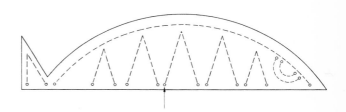

Fish

An interesting, decorative plaque, somewhat more difficult to form but a fine piece to have accomplished! Cut with a chisel, following the diagram, it is cleverly forged of one single piece of iron and mounted in a simple band frame.

Decorative flat-iron hinge extension arms.

Ornamental Door Knocker

This handsome door knocker is a real heritage piece to enhance your home. Made of 5/8″ round iron rod, it is thickened and forged in two pieces. The back plate is made of 1/8″ x 1 3/16″ flat iron, split into three sections which are forged into shape. The two outside arms have small loops to support the knocker. The assembled piece is attached to the door by two double pointed "staples" and the lower, pointed rivet at the base of the back plate.

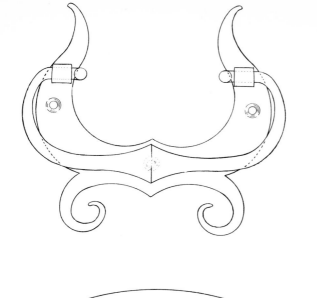

Furniture Hardware

Handsome forged iron fittings increase the value of furniture as well as enriching the appearance of any wooden chest, large or small. These drawings are only suggestions to guide the beginner in creating individual patterns using the methods he has now perfected with practice.

Flat iron $\frac{1}{8}''$ x $1''$ can be used effectively. The most important technique is splitting the material with the chisel. Any holes for nails are made with a mandrel in the heated iron.

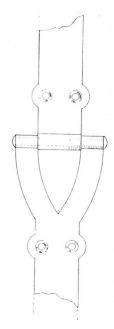

Hinge.

Surface Treatment of Forged Articles

The best treatment for the surface of forged iron objects is a *black oxide coating*.

The piece is warmed to about 572° F., and is then covered with a thin layer of linseed oil, smeared on with a thick wad of old cloth. Heat the article again, and rub over it a few more times with the same oiled cloth. Finally, dry it with a clean cloth.

After this treatment the iron will take on a black, silky surface appearance. Now you can polish it a little with an emery cloth, and lastly, apply lacquer or beeswax (dissolved in turpentine).

The treatment is certainly not difficult, however the warm and burning oil smells quite badly, thus this step should be done out of doors, if possible. There is a commercial finish, now available, which can simply be painted on.

Part 5

Further Examples

"Witches' cauldron"
made of iron.

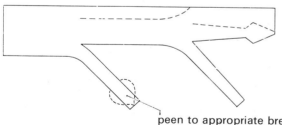

peen to appropriate breadth.

Hinge

Split the metal with a hot chisel according to the diagram. Surfacing should be done cold. The leaf-shaped terminals are peened with the back of the hammer. All sinkings are done with a ball-headed stamp. Metal $2\frac{3}{8}'' \times 2\frac{3}{8}''$.

Lamp

A lamp may be made of copper, brass or any other readily obtainable metal. The sheet should be about $\frac{1}{16}''$ thick. All the joints are riveted.

It is advisable to begin at the bottom. You will see from the diagram that the four corner supports are made of strips bent to a right angle and riveted to the base plate. Make sure all the angles are identical. At the top of these supports, crosswise angle irons are then riveted on.

The roof is made in one piece as in diagram 2.

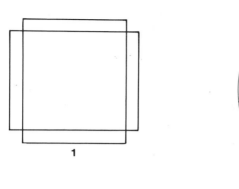

1

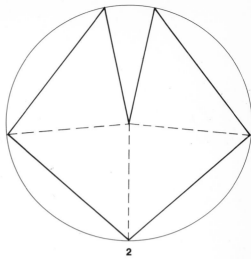

2

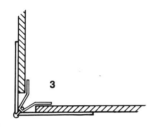

3

Draw a circle, the size of which you can decide by experiment, on a piece of paper. Cut out of it a triangle representing the height of the roof. Divide the remaining circumference into four equal parts. Now the outspread roof can be bent along the dotted lines, shown in diagram 2. The joins can then be soldered or riveted with the help of a thin.

piece of backing. The roof is secured with two screws so that it can be easily removed when the bulb is changed. On the inside of each corner support, rivet two thin metal strips to hold the glass in place, diagram 3.

If the lamp is to hang outside the house a special lamp-holder must be used. An ordinary lamp-holder is quite all right for indoors.

Lampstand

Height 5½″ approximately. The stand is made of ⅛″ sheet iron and the lamp-holder of ¼″ iron pipe with external thread and screws at the bottom and ⅜″ internal thread for the lamp-holder at the top.

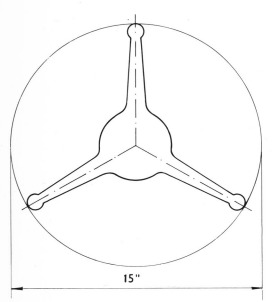

15″

Chandelier

The diameter of this chandelier is 11¾″ and the material for the ring measures 1¼″ x ⅛″. The candlesticks can be secured as follows: at the points of attachment two slots are made in the ring, dividing it horizontally into three equal sections, of which the top and bottom are bent inwards and the central one outwards. A square mandrel is then used to shape the hole so that three corners of the candlestick come on the outside. Alternatively the candlesticks can simply be riveted to the ring.

The holes for chains and leaf terminals are punched out with a semi-circular mandrel. The tapered candlesticks are made of ½″ iron bar, split at the top so that the bowls fit firmly for riveting. The candle-cups are made of ¾″ thin-walled pipe and soldered in place. The chains are of ⅛″ iron wire.

Horse and Bull

Length of horse and bull 7⅞" approximately.

The technique necessary here is welding and must be used with great care.

The horse is made from two ¼" iron plates, cut with an oxyacetylene cutter. The two halves are shaped concavely and roughly forged before being welded together along the back. Since the position of the right and left legs is different, the two sides will be different when cut out. The hairs of the mane are inserted into drilled holes and hard-soldered.

The bull is made in the same way as the horse.

Owl

The owl is made with ⅛″ sheet iron. The white areas are produced by perforating the sheet so that the background shows through. This is made of roughly plastered chipboard.

Fish

These forged fish are made up of different sections soldered together and mounted on plastered chipboard.

Crow

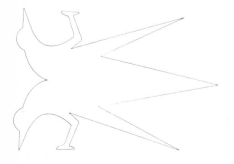

As the metal pattern is bent in half to form the bird's body, the sheet will split from back to beak, see drawing. The joint thus formed must be welded or hard-soldered. 1/8″ sheet is used.

Flock of Birds

First make thick paper models of the birds. Each bird consists of two halves which are welded or soldered together. The birds are made up in various shapes, producing a livelier image. They are linked together by hard-soldering.

Adam and Eve

Height 15¾″ approximately.

This piece of forging is one of the most difficult in the book and calls for very great skill.

The bodies are made of ¾″ iron bars. Adam's legs are forged from 1″ x ⅜″ flat iron bar and Eve's from ½″ rod. The tree is forged from 1¼″ x ¼″ flat iron bar. The leaves are soldered to a small section of tube and then joined on to the tree. The base is a 2¾″ x ½″ piece of flat iron.

Oxen

Length 10″ approximately.

The material is 1″ rod, flattened on two sides. The legs are of ½″ and the horns of ¼″ rod, hard-soldered to body and head respectively.

Tree Trunks

In wrought-iron work you must be very
determined as far as simplification of the
design is concerned. By varying the sizes of
materials and making a decorative combination of shapes good results can be obtained.

The work illustrated on these pages was done by
pupils at Steneby School.

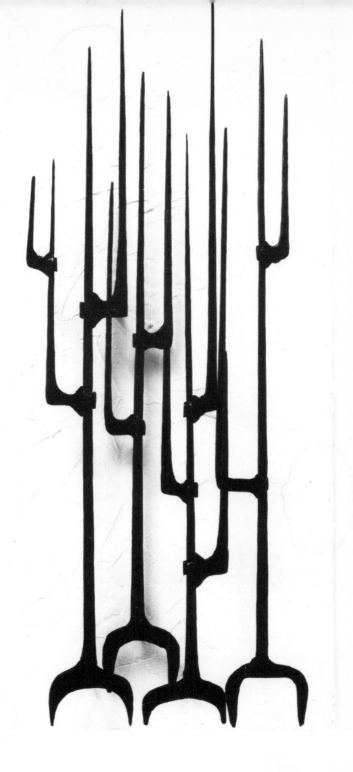